D1126496

WHEN BEING GOOD ISN'T GOOD ENOUGH

WITHDRAWN

3 3503 00058 7810

WHEN BEING GOOD ISN'T GOOD ENOUGH

Stephen Brown

 State Library of Ohio

SEO Library Center
40780 SR 821 * Caldwell, OH 43724

THOMAS NELSON PUBLISHERS
Nashville

The names of individuals whose stories appear in the book have
been changed to protect their privacy.

Copyright © 1990 by Stephen Brown

All rights reserved.
Written permission must be secured from the publisher to use
or reproduce any part of this book, except for brief quotations
in critical reviews or articles.

Published in Nashville, Tennessee,
by Thomas Nelson, Inc., and distributed in Canada
by Lawson Falle, Ltd., Cambridge, Ontario.

Printed in the United States of America.

Scripture quotations are from
THE NEW KING JAMES VERSION of the Bible.
Copyright © 1979, 1980, 1982, Thomas Nelson, Inc., Publishers.

Library of Congress Cataloging-in-Publication Data

Brown, Stephen W.
    When being good isn't good enough / Stephen Brown.
        p.   cm.
    Includes bibliographical references.
    ISBN 0-8407-7613-6 :
    1. Grace (Theology)   2. Faith.   3. Good works (Theology)
4. Christian life—Presbyterian authors.   I. Title.
BT761.2.B76   1990
234—dc20   90-31784
                                                       CIP

90–08619

DEDICATION

*To my brothers and sisters
who make up the congregation of
the Key Biscayne Presbyterian Church,
who give their pastor
the permission to be free.*

CONTENTS

Part Three:
IF JESUS HAS SET ME FREE, WHY DO I FEEL SO BOUND?

INTRODUCTION

Christian institutions in America are in trouble. If you haven't noticed, you haven't been paying attention.

When Francis Schaeffer first pointed out that we were living in a post-Christian era, those of us in the United States, while nodding in his direction, didn't believe it for a moment. After all, our churches were full, the impact of radio and television ministries was astounding, and we were finally achieving the political power we had long sought. How could anybody even suggest that things were bad when they appeared so good? What about all that money and power and acceptance?

Our people were everywhere, our books were best sellers, and our magazines were touching hundreds of thousands of people with the message of the Bible. Our president was in the White House and our agenda, for the first time ever, was possible. And then somebody turned the lights out.

It started slowly. It was only a small scandal. Never mind, we didn't expect everything and everybody to be perfect. And then another one. And another. Pretty soon it was an avalanche, and we were reeling from its impact. Our political power began to crumble. Our friends weren't our friends any more, and our enemies were celebrating. The criticism directed at evangelical Christians became strident, the laughter shrill, and the wounds deep.

There are dangers in success. We have discovered those dangers and we have been hurt. But there are also dangers in apparent failure. This book is about one of those dangers.

As the superficial walls of our success seem to crumble, committed leaders are raising their voices in alarm, calling for renewed obedience, discipline, repentance, and holiness. That is as it ought to be.

The danger is that the obedience could become a new legalism. You see, sometimes discipline is only a way to seize power, repentance only a worldly sorrow that leads to death, and holiness only another name for Pharisaism.

The problem is that our panic mode causes imprudent statements and actions. It is very important, it seems to me, that we go before the throne and do some checking. If we take the time to do that, we will find that there is no perspiration on God's upper lip. He hasn't been surprised by anything that has happened and I suspect has arranged it to teach us some much-needed lessons.

The good news of the gospel is still the good news. Our problems didn't come because we made it too good. Our problems came because *we didn't make it good enough.*

The message of the gospel is a message of freedom. Obedience and holiness are the result of that freedom, not the cause of it. If we ever get that backwards (and that is the danger of the present crisis), we will build new empires that God will once again have to destroy.

This book is an effort to remind Christians about the good news. A Nazarene carpenter went to a lot of trouble to "set the prisoners free," and we dare not ignore the price He paid nor spurn the gift He offers.

The sound of the hammer driving nails into His hands

and feet was a horrible sound—until someone checked the grave and saw that it was empty. Then we listened again. It had become the sound of freedom.

"Therefore if the Son makes you free, you shall be free indeed" (John 8:36).

Part One
FREEDOM AND GRACE: THE MISSING CHORD

CHAPTER 1

THE LAUGHTER OF GOD

(An Unexpected Sound)

"Now there were in the same country shepherds living out in the fields, keeping watch over their flock by night. And behold, an angel of the Lord stood before them, and the glory of the Lord shone around them, and they were greatly afraid. Then the angel said to them, 'Do not be afraid, for behold, I bring you good tidings of great joy which will be to all people. For there is born to you this day in the city of David a Savior, who is Christ the Lord.'"

Luke 2:8–11

Something is missing in the family of Christ.

It isn't that we aren't doing things right, that we aren't trying, that we don't care. It isn't that we have ignored God's commandments or been unfaithful to Christ; it isn't that we have become apostate. I spend a considerable portion of my time traveling around the country and for the most part God's people, with, of course, some significant and noteworthy exceptions, are doing what they ought to do.

But something is still missing. Nobody talks about it, but we all know it. Most of us have an "emperor-has-no-clothes" agreement with one another not to have seminars on the subject or to bring it up in committee meetings. But, nevertheless, we know. And when we aren't busy doing the right things for God, the void haunts us.

Something is missing. It's missing from our conferences, our churches, and, most tragic, it is missing from our lives.

At various times in my life I thought I had identified what it was. If we were just more holy, I thought, then God would do a great thing in the church. So I preached and taught holiness and tried to live it as best I could. We got more holy. But something was still missing. I asked myself, *Is that all there is?*

Maybe we needed to open ourselves to a new outpouring of signs and wonders. I read all the books and felt the excitement. We began having healing services in our congregation and God, in His mercy and love, granted some wonderful answers to our prayers. Still, something was missing, and the question remained on the back burner of my mind: *Is this all there is?*

Some folks told me I needed to be baptized in the Holy Spirit. I didn't like the words, but the reality made sense. After all, the Holy Spirit could give power, and that certainly was missing and needed. I tried. I really tried. I prayed and asked God to give me all He wanted for me. And then I was accepted by those who were "Spirit-filled."

And in that acceptance there was honesty. After all, we were family and we understood because we were Spirit-filled Christians. But when we were honest we often asked: *Is that all there is?*

Maybe the missing ingredient was doctrine. I became a five-point Calvinist and learned to repeat the Westminster Confession backwards. I preached it and taught it and we became doctrinally pure. But I looked into the eyes of those who had walked with me in our doctrinal purity, and I could see the same question: *Is that all there is?*

Maybe if we reached out more to the poor and the homeless or emphasized missions more or set up new dynamic programs of evangelism, or got into church growth—maybe then we would finally have the key. I tried them all.

But when we were tired—and we were often tired—the question still haunted us: *Is that all there is?*

I am writing this book after a long search—not because I have finally found the secret behind the secret but because the older I get the more I realize that Jesus really did come to "set the prisoners free." The more I think about and walk in that freedom, the more I have discovered the exquisite joy in following Him. I am just a beggar telling other beggars where I found bread . . . and this beggar is still sometimes hungry but he, at least, knows where the bread is.

Don't get me wrong. I still believe that Christ calls His people to holiness. I still believe that God's Spirit is the source of great power. I still believe that doctrine is vitally important and that missions, evangelism, and compassion are essential to the spiritual growth of believers.

But of late I have found something most of us, myself included, have missed: the laughter which comes from the freedom Christ gives us.

This book is about that laughter, and it's written to those for whom the good news has not been very good news for a long time.

I have a secret I'm going to share with you. As I have worked on this book late at night or early in the morning, I have sometimes paused to rest and think awhile. And in those quiet moments when the typewriter's clack was silent and no one was around to interrupt, I could hear laughter.

And then I knew what was missing.

THE CONTAGIOUS LAUGHTER OF GOD

When Jesus came something new happened. In fact, it was so incredibly new people almost missed it; they didn't expect it.

God laughed—not with the laughter of cynicism, judgment, derision, or sarcasm—but with the free, infectious, joyful laughter of the sovereign Ruler of the universe.

We didn't expect God to laugh that way. We expected Him to be angry, because we knew He had every reason to be angry. We expected Him to bring down justice on the injustice of His world, because we knew Him to be a just God. We expected Him to wipe out the whole mess and start all over. No one would have blamed Him. We expected lightning, wrath, intimidation, and a fearful display of power. We could have understood that.

. . . But laughter? Nobody expected laughter—free, gentle, accepting, and loving. That's what the incarnation of Christ is all about, and when we fail to see it that way, or when we proclaim it in any other way, we miss the whole point.

You will remember from Luke 4 Jesus' teaching in the synagogue of His home town. After reading a portion of the prophet Isaiah, He said a startling thing: "Today this Scripture is fulfilled in your hearing" (Luke 4:21).

Let me give you the entire quote from Isaiah 61:1–3:

> The Spirit of the Lord GOD is upon Me,
> Because the LORD has anointed Me
> To preach good tidings to the poor;
> He has sent Me to heal the brokenhearted,
> To proclaim liberty to the captives,
> And the opening of the prison to those who are bound;
> To proclaim the acceptable year of the LORD,
> And the day of vengeance of our God;
> To comfort all who mourn,
> To console those who mourn in Zion,
> To give them beauty for ashes,
> The oil of joy for mourning,
> The garment of praise for the spirit of heaviness;
> That they may be called trees of righteousness,
> The planting of the LORD, that He may be glorified.

Do you see it? For thousands of years men and women had looked into the heavens and asked, Is there a God? If so, what is He like? Does He care about us? Does He love us? Is He a monster? What does He require? Will He never reveal Himself? Does He take delight in our pain? Where is He? Why won't He tell us His requirements?

And then the laughter of God. . . .

"In the beginning was the Word, and the Word was with God, and the Word was God. He was in the beginning with God. All things were made through Him, and without Him nothing was made that was made. In Him was life, and the life was the light of men. . . . And the Word became flesh and dwelt among us, and we beheld His glory, the glory as of the only begotten of the Father, full of grace and truth" (John 1:1–5; 14).

Now we can begin to see some of what God was doing in the Incarnation. He was saying, "You people have it all wrong!"

Why was Jesus so angry at the Pharisees and the scribes? Because He had gone to a lot of trouble to give them some very good news about forgiveness, acceptance, and freedom. And they kept getting it wrong. Toscanini, who apologized to the symphony orchestra he was directing for having blown up, said, "The trouble is that God keeps telling me how the music is to be played, and you—you keep getting in the way."

Jesus said the same thing to the religious leaders of His day: "The Father keeps telling me how the music is to be played, and you—you keep getting in the way."

Genuine Christians ought to laugh a lot. In fact, Christians are the only people in the world who have anything to laugh about because God laughed first. And His laughter is contagious. One of the sure signs of God's presence in the midst of His people is the laughter of His people. Let me show you why.

The Forgiven Laugh

First, laughter and forgiveness go together.

Jesus died for our sin on a cross. He was the substitute for us, the sacrificial Lamb of God, bearing the penalty for our sin. "But this Man, after He had offered one sacrifice for sins forever, sat down at the right hand of God, from that time waiting till His enemies are made His footstool. For by one offering He has perfected forever those who are being sanctified" (Heb. 10:12–14).

What does that mean? It means you are covered and nobody is keeping score.

Early in my ministry I counseled a woman who, some twenty years before, had been unfaithful to her husband. For years that sin had haunted her. I was the first person she had ever told about it. After we talked and prayed for a long time, I recommended she tell her husband. (That, by the way, isn't always the advice I give. In this case, I knew the woman's husband and knew that her revelation, after the initial shock, would probably strengthen their marriage.) It wasn't easy for her, but she promised she would tell him. "Pastor," she said, "I trust you enough to do what you ask, but if my marriage falls apart as a result, I want you to know that I'm going to blame you." She didn't smile when she said that, either.

That's when I commenced to pray with a high degree of seriousness. (I pray best when I'm scared.) "Father," I prayed, "if I gave her dumb advice, forgive me and clean up my mess."

I saw her the next day, and she looked fifteen years younger. "What happened?" I asked. "When I told him," she exclaimed, "he replied that he had known about the incident for twenty years and was just waiting for me to tell him so he could tell me how much he loved me!" And then she started to laugh. "He forgave me twenty years ago, and I've been needlessly carrying all this guilt for all these years!"

Perhaps you are like the woman who had been forgiven and didn't know it. I am going to be talking a lot about sin and guilt in this book, but for now, let me suggest that you go to the Father and tell Him your sin. You will hear what He has said to so many others: "Child, didn't you know that I already forgave you?" Remember too that the laughter you hear comes from God's people who have been forgiven.

The Motivated Laugh

Not only do laughter and forgiveness go together, but laughter and motivation go together too.

You may not believe this, but with all my heart I want to be a good and faithful servant of Christ. I'll bet you do too. After some twenty-five years as a pastor I have found that the problem in the church is not that people don't want to be good, but that they want to be good and can't.

When I talk about freedom and grace and how God has destroyed the curse of the law, people tell me I'm treading on dangerous ground. "Steve," they admonish, "if you keep talking like that, Christians are going to go out and do what they want." Good. I still maintain that most Christians, if they did what they wanted, would be faithful. I have never heard a single Christian say, "Now that I'm forgiven I can be as bad as I want." (Of course, that kind of Christian may be somewhere. I've read about them in a lot of books and heard about them in a lot of sermons. I just can't find them. Perhaps there is one Christian like that. If any of you can find him, please tell him to stop. He's doing a lot of damage.)

When St. Augustine said, "Love *God*, and do as you please,"[1] he was getting close to God's secret of living the Christian life. At the risk of correcting Augustine (which is highly presumptuous) let me say he got it wrong. He should have said, "Let God love you deeply and completely, and then do as you please."

The problem is not "what we please." Because He has loved us so deeply and completely, Christians really do please to please God. The problem is that we so often fail in our efforts to please Him. Isn't that bad?

No. That's good! Jesus said, "Blessed are those who hunger and thirst for righteousness, for they shall be filled" (Matt. 5:6).

Let me give you a principle: Anticipating a promised reality is grounds for rejoicing in that reality. Jesus has promised that if you have a hunger and thirst for goodness, you will at some point be good. Because He promised, and because all His promises are fulfilled, you can rejoice as if you had already become good. If you know you're going to get something, you can rejoice almost as much as if you had it.

I have determined that after I write two more pages on this book I'm going to the refrigerator and get a dish of ice cream. That is an absolute promise I have made to myself. Just the thought of the ice cream makes my slaving over this typewriter bearable. Have I eaten the ice cream? No. Is the ice cream in the refrigerator? Yes. I checked. Is it mine yet? No, but it's going to be. The fact that it will be mine gives me a wonderful sense of joy. This rather pedestrian illustration tells us exactly the position of the Christian who has a desire to be good.

Evangelical Christians debate about how we can be assured of salvation. Some say the only way we can be assured of our salvation is to persevere in obedience, and as we obey, we will know we belong to Christ. (Detractors of this particular view call it works salvation.) Others say we can rest on the promise Jesus gave when we were saved; that is, "I accepted the gift of salvation when it was freely offered, and God doesn't lie. Therefore, I am saved." (Detractors of this view call it easy believism.) Still others say we can't know we have salvation—all we can do is hope and keep on trucking. When the game is over God will tell us whether or not we are saved. (Detractors of this view call it daisy salvation: He loves me, He loves me not; He loves me, He loves me not.)

Now, with as much humility as I can possibly muster, I'm going to settle the arguments: The way we are assured of salvation is to check and see if we desire to obey God. Please note: I did not say that you had to obey God 100 percent of the time—only that you have to want to. If you want obedience, you've got salvation. Scripture says, "Beloved, now we are children of God; and it has not yet been revealed that we shall be, but we know that when He is revealed, we shall be like Him, for we shall see Him as He is. And everyone who has this hope in Him purifies himself, just as He is pure" (1 John 3:2–3).

Do you see what John is saying? He is saying that the confirmation of your salvation is not in your being like Jesus now but in the hope you have of being like Jesus in heaven. When John gives us a future promise of being like Jesus (i.e., obedient) our desire for the fulfillment of that promise is not only the assurance of our salvation, it is the motivation (i.e., purifies himself) toward the fulfillment of the reality.

We'll talk about it again, but for now the laughter we hear is the laughter of those who have been motivated to goodness. You see, just as hunger presupposes food, and thirst presupposes water, a desire for goodness presupposes its reality.

The Successful Laugh

Third, not only does laughter go with forgiveness and motivation, but laughter and success go together too.

I am writing this on a Monday after the Sunday the Houston Oilers decimated the Miami Dolphins 39 to 7. Everybody expected Miami to win, and instead they suffered the most lopsided defeat in nine years. My friend Edwin Pope, sports editor of the *Miami Herald,* wrote about Miami quarterback Dan Marino's failure to play up to his normal high standards: "Marino, the man you could honestly say did most to lose the game, absolutely must find his stride both physically and mentally. He must create the rhythm and heart of the whole team. . . . Nothing will succeed if Marino doesn't. . . . He's where it starts. He has to pull them out of this funk."

I watched Marino being interviewed after the game. He was down, ashamed, and apologetic.

In your Christian life, have you ever felt like Marino? You tried. You really tried, but in the end you failed. You really wanted to do better, but you only did worse and you didn't know how to fix it. Maybe you considered giving up completely. You said to yourself, "I'll never get it right. I'm probably not a Christian at all."

Rules and regulations are Satan's way of reminding Christians that they have failed. But even worse, rules and regulations are the reason we do fail.

Let me give you a wonderful secret, the basic secret of this entire book. In fact, if you understand this, you don't need to read any further: When success isn't the issue, success becomes the reality.

C. S. Lewis had a wonderful lecture titled, "The Inner Ring," in which he spoke about how most of us wanted to be a part of the "in group" and would, in fact, do almost anything to achieve that end. He suggested that we forget our goal and concentrate on something else. He wrote:

> The quest of the Inner Ring will break your hearts unless you break it. But if you break it, a surprising result will follow. If in your working hours you make the work your end, you will presently find yourself all unawares inside the only circle in your profession that really matters. You will be one of the sound craftsmen, and other sound craftsmen will know it.[2]

In other words, success is always a side benefit of something else. You can apply that principle to lots of life's desires, but this book is about freedom, so let me show you how it works there.

Holiness and righteousness is the desire of every Christian. Many Christians say, "I'm going to be holy and righteous even if it kills me." And it usually does. But, and here is the exciting thing: Holiness and righteousness have already been achieved for you by Christ. When you stand before the Father, He sees you as holy and righteous because of the blood of His Son. You are, in fact, justified before God because of the cross.

That is a cold hard fact; you don't have to try so much anymore to be holy and righteous. You are now free to fail and, more importantly, free to allow Him to love you and to love Him back. You enter a relationship, not between a criminal and a policeman, but between a loving Father and His child. When you enjoy that relationship something wonderful happens: You find holiness and righteousness comes tagging along behind. You find that you, almost without knowing it, are in a process that makes you increasingly more holy and righteous.

This is the message. Obedience doesn't lead to freedom. *Freedom leads to obedience.* If that is backwards you lose both your freedom and eventually your obedience.

What you are going to read isn't about success or obedience—it's about freedom. It's not about a system—it's about the person of Jesus, who said, "If the Son makes you free, you shall be free indeed" (John 8:36).

A few years ago, *The Anatomy of an Illness* told how a man cured himself of cancer by laughing his way to health. He watched funny movies, read funny books, and listened to funny comedians. And then he got well.

That's how God's people get well too. If you listen you can hear them laugh the laughter of freedom, the laughter of the redeemed.

CHAPTER 2

THE
MUSIC
OF
FREEDOM
(The Boy Who Loved Music)

*"The elders have ceased gathering at the gate,
and the young men from their music. The
joy of our heart has ceased; our dance
has turned into mourning."*
Lamentations 5:14–15

Before we go any further in our discussion of freedom and grace I want to tell you a story. It is not fiction. Fiction is the telling of a story that is not true in a way that makes it seem true. The story I am going to tell is true, but its truth is deeper than the story. It is myth in the deeper sense of the word.

Some say that parables are closer to truth than polemics and that stories tell more than sermons. Or to put it another way, myth sometimes touches a deeper truth in us than philosophy. I suspect that is particularly true when presenting fairly radical ideas.

As you continue to read this book, you may grow confused and perhaps a little angry. You may think that I have gone off the "deep end" or that I have become a heretic. You may even find yourself wishing that the things I have said were true, but you are afraid to believe them because nothing could be that good!

On those occasions I want you to read this story again. In it you will find the essence of this book and, without sounding presumptuous, the essence of the Christian faith. Now relax and let me tell the story.

There once was a little boy named Ebed. Ebed had music in his heart, but he wanted it in his hands. He wanted to play the piano. In fact, he wanted to play the piano more than anything in the world. No one knew it, of course. Boys aren't supposed to play the piano; they're supposed to fish and camp and play sports. Ebed liked all those things, but more than anything he wanted to play the piano.

But Ebed's family couldn't afford piano lessons for him. So when his friends talked about learning to play the piano, Ebbie would laugh and make fun of them.

"Playing the piano," he would say, "is for girls. It's more fun to play ball. Pretty soon you guys will be wearing dresses and carrying purses!" And then Ebbie would walk off with a smirk on his face. But inside he knew the truth. More than anything in the world, he wanted to play the piano.

Sometimes when no one was around he would sit down at the piano at school and try to play. He really wasn't that bad for someone who had never had a lesson. In fact, his untutored playing made Ebbie think that he might have talent.

One day at the local ice cream parlor Ebbie noticed his friends and their piano teacher eating ice cream and laughing together. It was obvious to Ebbie that the piano teacher not only taught his students to play the piano but was also their friend. They, of course, didn't see Ebbie standing by the door. They were too absorbed in one another. Ebbie stood there for the longest time, afraid they would notice him, but also, in a strange way, afraid they wouldn't.

After a while Ebbie left the ice cream parlor. He felt very sad. He had kept up a good front in the parlor, but if anyone had noticed him, they would have noticed the tears welling up in his eyes. Ebbie ran down to the lake, where he went sometimes when he wanted to be alone. Once he was sure nobody was around, he sat down on a rock and began to cry.

Ebbie cried and thought for a long time. He thought about how much he wanted to play the piano, and he thought about the piano teacher. He knew his family was poor and there were some things he just couldn't have. But, still, it would be nice to have a friend like the piano teacher.

All of a sudden Ebbie heard a sound behind him. Turning quickly, he found to his horror that the piano teacher was standing there, smiling at him.

"Where did you come from?" Ebbie asked more harshly than he intended.

"I noticed you at the ice cream parlor," the piano teacher replied. "You looked lonely and I thought I would follow you. Do you mind if I sit down for a while?"

"Suit yourself," Ebbie said, "but I did come here to be alone, and I didn't invite you."

The piano teacher sat down on the same rock with Ebbie and for a long time didn't say a word. When the teacher did speak, his voice was soft and understanding.

"Ebed, would you like to play the piano?"

"What makes you think that? The piano is for girls and . . ." Ebbie's voice trailed off as he looked into the piano teacher's eyes. He couldn't lie. "Yes," Ebbie admitted slowly, "I would like to play the piano. In fact, sir, I have always wanted to play the piano, but I don't have the money to pay for lessons."

"Well, maybe I can do something to help."

"Yeah," Ebbie responded, "like what?"

"Well, I could be your friend. Friends don't charge for helping. If I was your friend, I could teach you to play the piano."

"That would be great!" Ebbie shouted, jumping up. In his excitement, he almost fell off the rock into the lake. But the piano teacher caught Ebbie just in time, and they both started to laugh. Ebbie couldn't remember a time he had laughed so hard.

"You know my name," Ebbie remarked. "I can't believe you know my name."

"Yes," the piano teacher agreed. "I've known your name for a long time."

"Well, if we're going to be friends, I guess I ought to know your name too."

"It's Immanuel," the teacher said. "But my best friends call me 'Manny.' I hope you will call me Manny too."

Ebbie decided that day he was going to be the best piano player who ever lived. "Others," he thought to himself, "don't think playing the piano is that important, but it's what I've wanted all my life. I will work and work until I'm the best piano student the teacher has, and he will be very proud of me."

But over the next few weeks, Ebbie found that playing the piano was not as easy as he had supposed. He had thought he would be well on his way after only a few lessons. Nobody, however, had told him about scales, the hours of practice, and the simple little tunes beginners have to play.

One day, after an extremely frustrating lesson, Ebbie turned to his teacher dejectedly. "I'll never get this right, Manny. I keep making the same mistakes over and over again. And I can see it in your eyes. You're about ready to give up on me, and I would understand. It's all my fault."

"Ebed." Immanuel's smile made his words almost unnecessary. "I will never give up on you. Friends don't give up on friends."

"What if I leave and don't come back?"

"Ebed, if you never came back, you are still my friend. I will always be here to give you lessons." And then with a grin Immanuel asked, "Do you still want to play the piano?"

"Of course, I want to play. I've always wanted to play, but nobody ever told me it was going to be this hard."

"Did I tell you it would be easy?"

"No sir."

"But I did say you would learn to play the piano, and that I would be your friend. We're working on the first, and the second will always be."

Immanuel sat down on the piano bench beside Ebbie. "Let's look at that piece you're working on."

Ebbie sheepishly got out his beginner's book and turned to "Twinkle, Twinkle Little Star." Ebbie blushed to show his teacher that he had gotten no further in the book.

"Play it for me," Immanuel said.

"But I can only play the treble line well."

"Doesn't matter. Play it for me anyway."

So Ebbie began to peck out the melody of "Twinkle, Twinkle Little Star." To be perfectly honest, the little star didn't twinkle very brightly. Ebbie kept missing notes and stopping often to make sure his fingers were in the right position. His rhythm was halting.

And then, to his surprise, Ebbie heard the most beautiful music he had ever heard. He looked to his right, Immanuel was adding to Ebbie's notes with his right hand. And then, without missing a beat, the piano teacher eased himself behind Ebbie, encircled Ebbie from behind with his arms, and added bass notes with his left hand as well! Ebbie continued to play his one-note melody, but now it sounded totally different.

Immanuel's melody wove into Ebbie's single line, transforming the simple melody into a complex symphony of sound. Ebbie was so fascinated that he almost forgot to keep playing. The harmonies, one on top of the other, soared in an increasingly complicated arrangement, sounding almost like an orchestra. Soon Ebbie was totally lost in the wonder and beauty of the music coming from the piano.

When Immanuel and Ebbie finished playing the piece, Ebbie felt tears stinging in his eyes, and through the tears he could see Immanuel smiling.

"We make pretty good music together," Immanuel said.

"You don't mean 'we,' do you?"

"Yes, Ebed. We made the music together. You did what you could, and I did the rest."

And then Immanuel invited Ebbie into his study. Over the weeks, Ebbie had enjoyed sitting and talking with Immanuel as much as he enjoyed learning to play the piano. In fact, if the truth were known, Ebbie enjoyed his time with Immanuel more than anything else in the world.

Immanuel lived in a large house close to the lake where he and Ebbie had first met. The house was almost overpowering in its size, and Ebbie always felt as if he were visiting the house of a great nobleman. At least, that is how he felt until Immanuel would answer the door. Then the cold, foreboding nature of the house was transformed by the presence of the teacher, and Ebbie felt he was visiting a good friend. *But then,* Ebbie thought often, *any place where Manny lived could not help but be wonderful.*

Immanuel was obviously quite wealthy and had wonderful taste. Ebbie was too young to understand the intricacies of interior design, but he was old enough to know that the house was "right." From the paintings which hung in the large entrance hall and the thick carpet on the floors to the grand piano on which Immanuel gave lessons, everything fit together and made Ebbie feel comfortable.

One thing always puzzled Ebbie, but whenever he was

with Manny, he forgot to ask him about it. Ebbie knew Manny had a lot of students, but Ebbie never saw any of them. In fact, when Ebbie was with Manny, there was never anyone else around and, even more surprising, Manny never seemed to be in a hurry to get to another lesson. Often Ebbie would expect his time to be limited, but it never was. Today wasn't any different—Manny seemed to have all the time in the world.

Immanuel's book-lined study, where they were now sitting, felt right to Ebbie too. The study was just off the studio where Immanuel taught his students. They were sitting in easy chairs, Immanuel's big frame filling his chair and Ebbie's small frame almost swallowed up by his. Ebbie's feet barely even touched the floor.

"Ebed," Immanuel began when they were settled, "you said I had made the music, or, at least, you insinuated it."

"Well," Ebbie replied, "you did make the music. You didn't need my single line to produce the kind of music you played today."

"That's true. I could make music by myself, but I have chosen not to do that. I have chosen instead to work with my friends and to help them make the music."

"Like today?"

"Yes, like today. You played as best you could, and I made up for the rest. Ebed, from now on it will be that way. Whenever you do what you can, I will make up for the lack. If you do nothing, I will still make up for the rest, and when you are older and play with far greater competence than you do now, you will still make some mistakes. Just remember that even then when others think you don't need me, I will still make up for the lack.

"And there is one other thing I want you to remember always. It won't mean a lot to you right now, but later you will think of it and be glad."

"What's that, Manny?" Ebbie asked, feeling a little uncomfortable.

"Don't look so pained," Immanuel laughed reassuringly. "It's good. I want you to always remember that you are my piano student. No matter where you go, no matter what you do, no matter how well or poorly you play the piano, you will always be my student. And Ebed, you can hang your hat on this: Someday, perhaps in another place and time, you will be able to play the piano exactly the way I play the piano. Even then, you will still be my student and my friend."

Then, to emphasize his words, Immanuel leaned forward. "Do you understand what I am saying?"

"I think I do," Ebbie responded.

"Ebed, I love you far more than you can possibly understand now. That will never, ever stop, no matter what else happens. I give my life for my students, and because of that they are always my students."

Ebbie thought a lot about what Manny had said to him that day. In fact, he never forgot it for the rest of his life.

But once he almost did.

As Ebbie continued piano lessons he found others teased him the same way he had teased Manny's students before he started taking piano lessons.

"Don't see you on the ballfield much any more," one boy snickered at him after school one day.

"I've been busy," Ebbie responded somewhat hesitantly.

"Playing the piano, huh?"

"Yeah, mostly."

"What have you become, some kind of fairy? You and the girls ought to get along just fine."

That was just the beginning. Soon, the other boys

joined in the teasing, making fun, not only of Ebbie's piano playing but of Ebbie's piano teacher as well. At first, Ebbie was angry at them, but after a while he started listening to and believing some of the things they said. Little boys need friends, and Ebbie was losing his rapidly.

Ebbie visited Manny's house less frequently, and he almost stopped practicing the piano altogether, even though he had been making genuine progress. The more he had practiced the better he had played. But now he was almost back to the level of a beginner. He was so ashamed that he finally stopped going to see Immanuel.

Weeks passed and, even though his friends had stopped making fun of him, Ebbie felt miserable. Sometimes he would look at the piano at school and think about playing, but it was just too costly. At night Ebbie would think about Manny and sometimes he would cry. He didn't know why he cried, but he did know that he missed Manny. Then, before finally falling asleep, Ebbie would make all kinds of promises to himself about getting back to the piano and going to see Manny. But when morning came he always forgot about the promises.

"Manny asked about you yesterday," Martus★, one of Immanuel's other piano students, told Ebbie one day at recess. "He said to tell you not to forget what he told you."

Ebbie didn't know what Martus meant until later that afternoon when he remembered that special talk in Manny's study. Ebbie felt the tears well up in his eyes. Instead of going home, he went to Immanuel's house.

"I've been expecting you," Immanuel said as he opened the door. "Are you ready for your next lesson?"

"But I haven't played in so many months." Ebbie

★Greek for "witness."

looked down and pretended to find something quite interesting in the rock floor on the porch.

"Doesn't matter. You are always my piano student, and that hasn't changed. You may have been a poor one for the past few months," Immanuel smiled, "but you *are* my student. Come on in, and we can begin where we left off."

It was the best piano lesson Ebbie had ever had. In fact, Ebbie thought at home later, *I'm almost glad I turned away from Manny and his piano lessons. If I had never turned away, I would never have known how much Immanuel loves me and how much he wants me to continue piano lessons.*

It was a growth experience for Ebbie. Whenever his friends teased him he would remember how he had caved in to their criticism and how Immanuel still loved him, and his sadness would be transformed into joy and thankfulness.

But the trouble Ebbie had with those who didn't understand the importance of playing the piano was minor compared to the trouble he had with his fellow piano students.

Ebbie thought that once he became a piano student he would become part of a family of musicians where everyone understood and helped each other play the piano better. It was not to be.

"You're doing it all wrong!" shouted a little girl who had overheard him practicing on the piano at school. "You're playing soft when you ought to be playing loud, and you're playing loud where you ought to be playing soft."

"Your rhythm is all off," criticized another student who had heard Ebbie play. "How do you ever expect to play the piano if you can't tell the difference between 4/4 and 3/4 time?"

"You hit three wrong notes," another exclaimed. "If

you don't start playing the right notes, you are going to disappoint the teacher. And after all he has done for you! The rest of us have been talking and we've decided that if you don't get better, you're going to shame all of us."

"If you are ever going to play the piano properly, you must practice at home, not at school," one of the students informed Ebbie one day after class.

"But I don't have a piano at home," protested Ebbie.

"Well, why don't you get your parents to buy you one?"

"We don't have the money. That's why."

There was a long silence, but Ebbie noticed a look of disdain on his fellow student's face as he walked away. He knew the boy felt that Ebbie should quit taking piano lessons if he couldn't afford a piano.

One afternoon when Ebbie had finished his lesson, Immanuel said to him, "Ebed, you seem sad. What's the matter?"

"Oh, nothing," Ebbie replied, betraying his words with the grimace on his face.

"The others bothering you?"

"Sometimes."

"They bother me too sometimes."

"But you don't hear all the things they say."

And then Immanuel smiled. "Ebbie, I know my students. The girl who told you that you needed to play soft when you are playing loud, and loud when you ought to be playing soft, is only criticizing you because she is doing so badly with her own lessons. The boy who criticized your rhythm hasn't been to a lesson in almost three months. He thinks if he points out your mistakes, people will not notice his own.

"The boy who told you about the wrong notes is so busy telling others about their wrong notes, he doesn't

41

have much time to play himself. If he played the piano very much, which he doesn't, he would probably hit more wrong notes than you do. The boy who told you to buy a piano with money you don't have has three pianos, but he hardly ever plays any of them. He thinks that having pretty pianos is more important than playing them. People always admire his pianos, and he thinks it's the same thing as admiring his piano playing.

"And the others who suggested that you were hurting the reputation of all the students are very insecure about their own piano playing. Your playing is different, and the other students don't like piano players who are different.

"And Ebbie, the comment about disappointing me isn't true. Never let another piano student tell you that you disappoint me. If I'm disappointed, I'll tell you. When I'm pleased, I'll tell you that too. But I am the only one who knows whether I'm disappointed or pleased."

Ebbie felt a whole lot better after Immanuel told him about the other students. In fact, he felt a little superior to the others. That is, until Immanuel said to him, "Ebbie, I'm telling you all this so you will remember that I have made you my student, even with your mistakes, because I love you. But I don't love you more than the others. The only reason I told you about them—and if I chose, I could tell them a lot about you—is so you will remember that there isn't a single piano student in the world who doesn't make some serious errors. Their problem is that they tried to pretend they were better than you.

"Now you know the truth. Remember it, and don't make their mistake. Remember how you forgot about me for so long? How you quit practicing and how I accepted you when you wanted to resume your lessons? Remember how I never stopped loving you? I will do the same for them. All my piano students are equal because they have the same teacher. You must never think you are better than the others just because you know the truth.

"And Ebbie, never forget that I make up the difference for them, just as I do for you."

After that, Ebbie loved Immanuel more than he ever had. When he walked away from the teacher's house, he felt free. He didn't have to pretend to be a wonderful piano student. Nor did he have to pretend not to care. He didn't have to point out the mistakes of the other students in order to feel better about himself; after all, the piano teacher loved all the piano students. All Ebed had to do was stay close to the piano teacher.

Every spring, Immanuel had a recital at his home for his students' parents. Ebbie had worked for weeks on his piece, and his mother had bought him a new suit with some money she had saved. Ebbie felt wonderful—until he got up to play.

When he started to walk toward the piano and saw all the people waiting for him to perform, he panicked. He wanted to run. But when he looked over at Immanuel, his teacher gave him a "thumbs up" sign. *No way am I going to disappoint Manny,* Ebbie thought.

But as Ebbie began to play, he forgot the music. He played the wrong notes. Once he even lost his place and had to start over. When Ebbie got up from the piano bench, he didn't dare look at the audience or his parents or, especially, Immanuel. He had wanted to do so much better. But instead, he had disappointed everyone.

Ebbie was so miserable he didn't notice that the audience was applauding. In fact, they applauded for almost five whole minutes, shouting "Encore! Encore!" Ebbie didn't hear it. He had already walked out the back door and headed down to the lake where he sat on his rock and cursed himself.

Hours passed and the night grew cold. Suddenly, Ebbie heard a rustle behind him, and he turned to find Immanuel standing there.

"I really botched it."

"Yes, you really botched it. But they didn't know."

"What do you mean, they didn't know? Of course they knew. I'm so ashamed. How can I ever face them again? And Manny, I'm even more ashamed to face you. You loved me. You trusted me. You taught me to play the piano, and I let you down. Please don't look at me that way, Manny. I don't believe I can stand it."

"Ebed," Manny said, taking an uninvited seat on the rock by the boy, "you misinterpret my look. I'm not disappointed in you. You must remember that I've been teaching piano for a long time—longer than you could possibly know. Do you think your performance surprised me?"

"Well, I guess not. But. . . ."

"No buts, child. Your vanity has been hurt, but you haven't failed me. Ebed, I love you. I've told you that, but you forgot."

"I guess I did," Ebbie whispered.

"And you forgot something else."

"What's that?"

"Remember, I told you I would always make up for your lack. I did that tonight."

"You mean. . . ."

"That's right. You didn't play as well as you will play some day, and perhaps you didn't play as well as you could have played. But you played, and I made up for the difference. The audience heard the music, not the mistakes!"

Ebbie jumped up and started to dance on the rock. Immanuel laughed heartily, but managed to caution Ebed,

"You are going to fall off this rock if you aren't careful, and I don't relish going swimming on this kind of night."

That night was one of the most important nights of Ebed's life, second only to the evening he had met Immanuel. Ebed began to practice playing the piano far more than he had previously.

In the years to come, Ebed botched some other concerts. Sometimes he got angry at Immanuel. Sometimes he thought about giving up on the whole thing, and he even walked away a few more times. But Immanuel was always there, loving him and helping him make music.

You might wonder what happened to the little boy. That's the best part.

Ebed grew up and became a world-class pianist. He came to be known, as one critic put it, as "the essence of perfection." In concert after concert, all over the world, Ebed played to standing-room-only audiences. When he finished a concert, after the applause had died away, Ebed would smile and remember that no one had heard his mistakes. Later he would always thank Immanuel for making up for the lack.

One evening after a concert in New York, when he was almost seventy years old, Ebed was dining with some friends when he felt a mild pain in his chest. He marked it up to indigestion, but as the evening wore on the pain became more and more acute. Halfway through dinner he collapsed, and his friends called an ambulance.

Ebed was only half conscious when they put him on the stretcher and placed him in the ambulance, but then he woke up. It was a strange kind of awake because he seemed to be looking at the whole scene in the ambulance from a different perspective. One of the attendants looked at the other and sighed, "We've lost him."

"You haven't lost me!" Ebed wanted to shout. "I'm right here!"

But before Ebed could speak the sound of a piano caught his ears—the most beautiful music he had ever heard! Turning around, he found himself at Immanuel's house. Well, maybe it wasn't Immanuel's house, but it looked the same, only even more beautiful than he remembered.

Drawn through the front door by the music, Ebed found Immanuel playing a magnificent concerto at the grand piano. Ebed listened, entranced.

When Immanuel finished, neither he nor Ebed spoke for a moment. Then, turning to Ebed, Immanuel broke the silence. "Now, it is your turn."

"Me?"

"Yes, you!" Immanuel laughed. "And I believe you are in for a surprise!"

Ebed sat down at the piano, and as he placed his hands on the keys, he felt a freedom and power he had never before felt. Every nuance, every note, every rhythm was perfect. The music soared and filled the room. Out of the corner of his eyes, Ebed could see Immanuel smiling, as a father smiles when his son performs perfectly. Ebed's heart beat excitedly.

"Ebed," Immanuel said softly, "now you play just the way I play."

"Yes," Ebed replied, smiling, "I know."

"And I have a new name for you, Ebed. Before, you have been called Ebed.* Now your name is Deror.* Now the music is yours forever. You are home."

---

*Ebed is Hebrew for "servant" or "slave." Deror is Hebrew for "liberty" or "freedom."

CHAPTER 3

FETTERS AND FREEDOM
(When Good Isn't Good Enough)

"O foolish Galatians!
Who has bewitched you . . . ?"
Galatians 3:1

Bishop William Quayle once gave a sermon for preachers in which he named observation as one of the major tasks of a preacher. He wrote:

> When this preacher comes to a Sunday in his journey through the week, people ask him, "Preacherman, where were you and what saw you while the workdays were sweating at their toil?" And then on this preacher we may say reverently, "He opened his mouth and taught them saying:" and there will be another though lesser Sermon on the Mount. And the auditors sit and sob and shout under their breath, and say with their helped hearts, "Preacher, saw you and heard you that? You were well employed. Go out and listen and look another week; but be very sure to come back and tell us what you heard and saw."[3]

Before I started work on this book, I wanted to make sure I reported accurately what I heard and saw. I wanted to be careful not to become some kind of Don Quixote, battling windmills. Too often in the church we try to fix things that aren't broken.

All of us have heard (and some of us have preached) sermons which dealt with problems that didn't exist. When the sermon was over we felt as if the preacher had masterfully solved a problem nobody had. Those kinds of sermons do one of two things: they either cause people to acquire problems they don't have or, they cause the more

WHEN BEING GOOD ISN'T GOOD ENOUGH

thoughtful listener to spend his or her next Sunday doing something more productive, like playing golf or sleeping.

For years, as a pastor and counselor, I have dealt with the lack of Christian freedom in myself and in others. Over and over again I have seen people, who ought to be joyful, free Christians, suffer a strange, unhealthy bondage to the world and to the opinions of other Christians.

When I was asked to write this book, I asked myself: *What if the problem is only with my perception? What if, like Freud, I have been dealing with sickness so long that I see everyone in light of that sickness? What if I have universalized something that is a problem only for a few individuals?*

IS SOMETHING MISSING?

You probably know the story of the psychiatrist who gave the Rorschach test to one of his clients. (The test consists of ten inkblots of varying designs with no reference to a particular scene or picture. The client interprets each of the inkblots.) This particular client responded to each inkblot with a rather lurid sexual description. After they had gone through a number of inkblots, the psychiatrist asked the client, "Do you mean that you see something sexual in every one of these?"

"Don't get upset with me, Doc," the client responded. "You're the one who owns the dirty pictures!"

I've wondered while writing this book if I am the one with the dirty pictures or if the problem is elsewhere. Is the lack of Christian freedom as great a problem as I perceive it to be?

What is my assessment of the problem? I see it in major, catastrophic proportions. Somewhere, somehow, the church has lost the excitement and joy of its message of freedom. The very thing that Jesus spoke against—the slavery of the Pharisees—has once again become the mark of the church, and I believe that Jesus is just as angry about it today as He was in the first century.

But what if I am wrong?

Before I started writing this book, I asked the people who listen to Key Life's national radio program to write me about what they had discovered about freedom. The response was overwhelming. I received so many letters I could have devoted the rest of the book to them. But let me share a few to show you the problem. See if you find yourself in their comments. If not, then you needn't read further. However, if you do find yourself, those you love, or the church in which you serve, this book may be the best thing to happen to you in years, because it will give you some accurate biblical information that could change your life.

A man in Washington state wrote that, as a boy, he had come to know Christ. He talked about the great difference Christ had made in his "growing up" years. As an adult, he lived in San Jose, California, and got involved in a very exciting Christian fellowship. He heard things he had never heard about obedience and about his responsibility as a Christian. "And, Steve," he wrote, "I really tried to conform to the Christianity I was being taught."

> My wife and I would attend seminars on anything Christian whenever we had the opportunity. After about two years and lots of seminars I changed on the outside, but the inside was not what I thought I had been promised in His Word. I made all sorts of commitments, but I soon broke the promises I had made to God, except the last one I made: I promised God that I would make no more promises. In frustration I looked to the Father and told Him I would not

read His Word anymore out of obligation. I would not commit to anything out of duty. My prayer would be spontaneous or not at all.

"Things didn't change overnight but now with room to work on me He began to show Himself. I am becoming free to pray and read the Bible again. Steve, I am not trying to say that now I live in blissful joy. You and I would know that I would be lying again. But I am free to fail now. I don't have to be a 'good Christian' anymore.

A pastor from Massachusetts who has for a number of years served a strongly disciplined (some would say legalistic) church and who himself was the perpetrator of most of the discipline, said, "I won't be here in another year. I just can't live this way. I thought I was doing right by adhering to the strong standards we maintain. But I have become the pastor of some of the sourest saints I have ever known . . . and I'm one of them."

A couple in Michigan wrote about their ministry with young people. They demonstrate the Korean style of the martial arts, and, once they have a crowd, talk about Christ. You can imagine the kind of criticism they receive from some Christians. "We have both," they wrote, "run the gamut of lifestyles beginning with having been raised in a very strict church in which we were involved in church activities eight days a week."

They described their four years of backsliding and the resultant guilt. Believe it or not, their way back to obedience was not through trying harder and achieving the victorious Christian life. On the contrary.

Someone gave this couple some tapes of my Bible teaching. The tapes were about freedom and forgiveness. They wrote,

Thank God, He did not give up on us! Our recent revelation through your cassettes that we are human and that God has already forgiven us is something we couldn't hear for so long. Either we were deaf, or were not being apprised of this gift. The sweet, sweet certainty that we now taste daily is the unalterable fact that we are forgiven for our sins. We are now walking with Him. Your philosophy has touched us deeply and the freedom we have experienced from God has made a great difference in our lives.

A woman in Arizona wrote that she was thinking of the way she was when she was young. She said,

My children were very small and I was trying to be a great mom, a great church member, and a great wife. I was not working out of the home, but that would have been a vacation compared to what I was trying to accomplish. In Sunday school I kept hearing the other members talk about their lives. Some said they prayed constantly, while ironing, washing, or mopping. They were thankful for all things.

"I tried being like those other women but finally gave up. Gradually I quit insisting that we all get up on Sunday morning to go to church. Trying to live up to the standards I thought others lived by almost destroyed me.

And then she met a missionary and was surprised by freedom. It is easy to understand, given her past experience, why this woman was rather wary of the missionaries. She had all the guilt she could handle. But the missionary, instead of criticizing and judging my correspondent, confessed her own weakness and lack of commitment. She writes, "I don't remember what she did, but I do remember she allowed me to see her weak and human side. And yet, with all her weakness, she was still serving Christ. It was a revelation in my life. I'm back now with Christ, and I'm a different person."

One young man wrote to me that he had to leave the ministry in order to experience the freedom of Christ. He grew up a minister's son and was taught the standards of the Christian faith. But he was never able to live up to those standards or, at least, live up to them as they were defined by his minister father. "Without going into detail about the years that followed, let it suffice to say that I lived in bondage."

He entered college as a pre-med major. He continued,

> I was still struggling to be a Christian and by that time I was even struggling to feel good about myself. I had become a good ball player in high school (by everyone else's standards) but I didn't feel good enough because I never seemed to attain the perfection that gained my dad's recognition. It wasn't that he punished me but, even when I played a good game, he would criticize areas that needed improvement. I worked so hard to get his approval. In the same way I was working to get my heavenly Father's approval.

Eventually, this young man decided that he had been called to the ministry. In reality he had come to the point where he felt that pleasing both of his fathers (one human and the other divine) required that he become very spiritual (and everyone knows that means becoming a pastor). He wrote, "Once in the ministry I thought things would change. Surely God would bless my ministry and I would have His approval."

But things didn't change. While he was quite successful in the ministry, he couldn't stand it any longer and left. He finally realized that he could never please either his Father in heaven or his father on earth.

Gratefully, my relationship with God began to change. About three years ago a man shared a scripture with me that God opened up in a new way. It was in John where Jesus says, 'I no longer call you servants, but friends.' I have begun to realize that even though I was God's since age eight, I was His as a servant. I was trying desperately to please the Master through doing what He commanded. Now I realize I am His friend too. Now, even though I desire to stay away from sin, what I do or don't do is not as important as knowing that our friendship can cope with my failures.

He didn't go back into the ministry, but the story has a happy ending.

I am a builder now and I really enjoy what I am doing. In fact, I felt so free that the other day when talking to a woman about Christ, for the first time in a long time, I didn't feel the need to orchestrate how I handled her situation. I was free to be obedient. Steve, I know I've just tasted freedom. There must be so much more to come. I crave for it and I hope that your book will help 'us' find it.

A woman from New Jersey wrote that when she became a Christian she was frightened by the good people she met. "I was convinced that I could never be as good or obedient or cooperative as they were. I left Christ and His church for a very long time. This apostasy wasn't any fault of theirs, but mine. I just didn't understand."

The thought of becoming a quiet, well behaved young lady when my natural personality was outspoken, energetic, and probably sometimes more than just a little rowdy, was something I could not bear. I love art, and not just pious pictures of bleeding saints and hovering angels (who, by the way, do not look like the fearsome champions of heaven that I believe they are). I love music and dancing and singing and laughing. In the beginning of my Christian life, I was certain that I would have to give all of that up. I had friends who did not dance, who had thrown out all of their rock music, and who followed the rules much better than I ever did or could. I tried for a long time to be like them and hated myself for not being able to stop being me! I rebelled to the limits of rebellion. I stayed away for ten years.

Her story is another happy ending.

It is a good thing that God is bigger than all of that or I would have never found my way back. In fact, I believe God found me and brought me back. . . . I realize that I limited God. A pretty ridiculous thing, wouldn't you say? I have also learned to forgive myself. I realize that I am what God made me and I now accept myself and the part of me that wants and needs to sing and dance and talk a blue streak. Obedience has a different meaning—a good one. Submissiveness is something I have chosen to do.

Not all the letters had a happy ending. Many revealed the continuing struggle of people who had yet to understand the meaning of freedom. A woman in Florida wrote:

I am so angry and frustrated because I feel like I'm trying to live in two worlds simultaneously and failing in both. I just can't be what Christian friends say I must. I can't always be smiling, up, walking with my head in the clouds, folding my hands, and saying, 'Praise the Lord!' I get depressed, scared, feel alone and angry, even at God! Then when these feelings subside I feel guilty.

I need freedom. I need a God who understands my feelings and isn't going to zap me with a lightning bolt because of them.

A thirty-five-year-old man who is a confirmed homosexual wrote:

I don't like who I am, and I want to be different. Please don't tell me to get with Christians. I tried to talk to people in the church and they can't deal with my sin. If they only knew how much I want to be free of this thing. I just don't know how. I became a Christian when I was sixteen, but nobody will believe me because of my sin. Maybe they are right.

Over and over people expressed their desire for freedom. From pastors and lay people across the country there was the honest admission that, while there is a lot of talk about freedom, there is very little of the real thing.

THE FREEDOM
TO BE A FRIEND

I could, of course, go on. These people are all discovering that freedom is not just another word for nothing left to lose—or maybe they have discovered that it is. Maybe they have lost (or tried) everything else. When you don't have anything else to lose, you discover something wonderful: You *are* free! The horrible effort to protect, rationalize, hide, and pretend is gone. All you have left is Jesus. Of course, you don't realize Jesus is all you need until Jesus is all you've got. When He is all you've got, then you know that He is all you need.

When I was at seminary, I took a course in liturgical worship. During one of our classes, the professor criticized a student for reading the Sanctus (the place in the liturgy that begins with "Holy, holy, holy") at the wrong time in the liturgy. "If we are ever going to be relevant to the people we serve in the church," the professor said, "it is necessary that the liturgy be right." (Actually, I think he said, "that the Sanctus be in the right place," but nobody would have said something that stupid.)

Most of us are just as mixed up as that professor. The Christian faith isn't about the Sanctus or liturgy or rules or religion or theology or doctrine or conformity or trying to please other people. The Christian faith is about a relationship with someone who loves you and who has given you the freedom to be His friend.

The further we get from that freedom, the further we get from New Testament Christianity and the more our Christianity resembles every other religion—merely a system for keeping the baser instincts of human nature in check. In other words, Christianity becomes a system of rules and regulations. If we live by them, our Christianity becomes pure drudgery with a vague hope that God will reward us in heaven for the drudgery. If we don't live by them, we either lie about it or give up altogether.

There is a third way to live the Christian life, and it is quite radical. Let's talk about it in the next chapter.

CHAPTER 4

SOME REVOLUTIONARY IDEAS
(The Radical Nature of Freedom)

*"Then Jesus said to those Jews who believed Him,
'If you abide in My word, you are My disciples
indeed. And you shall know the truth, and the truth
shall make you free. . . . Therefore if the Son
makes you free, you shall be free indeed.'"*
John 8:31–32, 36

The Christian faith is radical. In fact, if what you call "Christian" is not radical, then it is probably not Christian.

Those of us who have been around Christianity a long time have forgotten how radical our faith really is. In fact, that we believe it at all is a very cogent argument for its truth. Nobody in their right mind would make it up. Think about it.

We believe that there really is a God Who created the whole world for His purposes and that those purposes are being worked out in history. We believe this God is holy and righteous and rather frightening. While He is a Father, He is also a very dangerous Father.

(If I had made up a religion I would have created a God who was a little more, well, fatherly. I would have dreamed up a father like the one in the popular television series of the 1960s, "Father Knows Best," sort of like the father image about which Freud spoke.)

We believe that this God called a particular people, the Jews, who were wandering bedouins in the desert, and told them that He would be their God and they would be His people. The Jews were not educated, sophisticated, or great among the peoples of the earth. (If I had had anything to do with it, I would have picked the Egyptians or the Babylonians.)

How odd
For God
To choose
The Jews.

We believe that this same God who called this group of bedouins from the desert brought forth a Messiah from that people. We believe the Messiah was born in Bethlehem of Judea and that His legal father was a carpenter and his mother was a nobody. (If I had written the script, I would have picked a royal family in Europe.)

It is enough that we believe that the Messiah came from such a strange place and from such an obscure people, but there is more. We believe that this Messiah was the incarnation of God—that God Himself entered time and space as a Jew in Bethlehem, a small out-of-the-way town nobody ever heard of. We believe God, as the Messiah, walked our dirty roads and died as a common criminal. (If I had been creating the story, I would have had the Messiah born in one of the world's great cosmopolitan cities. I would have picked a heritage considerably less pedestrian. If I were dreaming up a world religion I would have stopped there. But God didn't stop there.)

We believe that after the Messiah died, a dead man got up and walked. And to compound the embarrassment, we believe He ascended to heaven and sat at the right hand of God the Father. (I would have picked something else with which to impress the world, something a little more believable.)

And then, to make matters worse, we believe that this little Jewish rabbi has become the measurement by which the world will be judged—that His horrible death is directly related to the forgiveness, meaning, and eternal life of His people. We believe that He died for us, and that someday He is going to return to clean up the mess.

If you believe all that, you'll believe anything!

Yet that is exactly what we believe. The very fact that we do believe it suggests that either we are crazy or it is true. That is not to suggest that the Christian faith is irrational. On the contrary, any informed Christian who has ever argued the Christian faith with a pagan, knows how silly and irrational unbelief is. It does mean, however, that the facts upon which our faith is built are so big and so unexpected that nobody would ever dream them up, and no one in his or her right mind would try to build a philosophy on something that unbelievable.

You see, the Christian faith is radical. If it were our idea, nobody would have believed it. But it isn't our idea. It's God's idea. Why? Because God is radical. It should be no surprise, then, that what is clearly taught in Scripture is radical. What you will find in the following chapters will, I believe, sound quite radical. I only ask you to hear me out. If you do, it is my prayer you will first be shocked. You will exclaim, "I don't believe he really said that! The Bible couldn't possibly teach that. It isn't what I thought at all."

After you are shocked, I pray you will become angry. I hope you will say, "He is a libertarian. The problem with our society is that we have lost our values, and this man is making it even worse. Easy believism is all it is. And he calls himself a man of God!"

Then I want you to be thoughtful. I hope you will say, "Wait just a minute. Maybe the Bible does say all that; maybe we are that free; maybe I have been bound all these years."

Finally, I pray that your laughter will join with mine—that you will find yourself excited and thankful for the freedom Christ has given you. I pray that you will say with the freed slave, "I'm free! I'm free! Thank God Almighty, I'm free at last!"

FREE IN CHRIST

Enough chitchat. What is the radical idea? Pay attention! The radical idea is this: If you are a Christian, you are free. No, I don't mean you are free with a number of ifs, ands, and buts. I mean you are really free. No disclaimer. No addendum. No qualifying points. You are free.

I didn't say it. Jesus did: "'If you abide in My word, you are My disciples indeed. And you shall know the truth, and the truth shall make you free. . . . Therefore if the Son makes you free, you shall be free indeed'" (John 8:31–32, 36). Freedom is a gift from the Son of God. If He says I'm free, that ought to settle it for me. And He does say it. So I dare anyone to say otherwise.

What does it mean to be free in Christ? It means we are free from the rules we thought bound us to God. It means we are free from the manipulation other Christians use to make us like them—free from having to fit into the world's mold, free to be different.

We are free from the slavery of religion and from the fear of rejection, alienation, and guilt. We are free from the fear of death. We are free from masks, free from the sham and pretense; free to doubt, free to risk, free to question. It means we are free to live every moment. But most of all, we are free to follow Christ, not because we have to but because we want to.

I know what you're thinking. I shouldn't have said all that. To be perfectly honest, I agree. I just read the list over and thought, *I think I'll tone that down a bit. Maybe it's somewhat radical. Perhaps I ought to bring it on a little more slowly or say it differently.* But, you see, I have this philosophy that comes from Ecclesiastes 9:10: "Whatever your hand finds to do, do it with all your might."

That means if you're going to follow Christ, don't pussyfoot around. Follow Him all the way. If you are going to be in trouble, really get into trouble. If you're going to steal, don't steal just a little bit. Go rob a bank. If you are going to play poker, don't bet pennies. If you're going to make a fool of yourself, don't hedge. Look like a real idiot or don't say anything! If you've decided to tell the truth, tell it all and then get out of the way.

Martin Luther said, "Be a sinner and sin mightily, but more mightily believe and rejoice in Christ."[4] I can identify with that.

I teach communications at Reformed Seminary in Jackson, Mississippi, and Orlando, Florida. In one of my classes in Jackson I was talking about the importance of risk, telling my students that if they had any doubts about saying something, they probably ought to say it. It's better to shock people than to put them to sleep.

I started to give examples of things I've said from my church pulpit in Miami—some which got me in trouble, and some which enabled people to see God. Dr. Gordon Reed, my dear friend and the head of the homiletics department at Reformed, was sitting in on my class. Raising his hand, he asked, "Steve, is it okay if I say something?" Given the fact that he is the department head, I told him he could say whatever he wanted. Turning to my class, he smiled and, with a twinkle in his eyes, he spoke in his soft southern drawl, "Boys, I appreciate what Steve has been saying, but none of that is gonna work north of Orlando."

Well, he had a point. I would probably be a whole lot better off if I listened to Gordon more than I do. But I just can't.

When I say you are free, every "But, Steve you don't

mean" is exactly what I do mean. That doesn't mean I'm necessarily comfortable with it all.

I am greatly concerned for the truth of what I teach. I live in fear that someone will misinterpret what I teach and make a horrible mess of their lives. I know that James 3:1 is true: "My brethren, let not many of you become teachers, knowing that we shall receive a stricter judgment." I am acutely aware that I'm going to have to report in someday—a frightening thought! I have nightmares about the Father saying, "Son, do you remember what you taught on that subject? Let me show you what happened as a result of your teaching."

In my nightmares, a gigantic screen is lowered just behind the throne and on it I see God's people devastated and hurt and unfaithful because of what I taught them. I wince, and something in me says, "Steve, don't say it that way. People will misunderstand. They'll go out and mess everything up. You'll hurt their witness. If you tell them they are free, they will become libertarian. They will take great license, and if there's anything we don't need today it is disobedient Christians."

But nevertheless, trembling, I must say it again: If you belong to Christ, you are really free. You are free, and I say it without disclaimers, without addendums, without qualifiers. Let me say it again: You are free! You are free! You are really free!!

There. I've said it again and I'm glad.

Dead to the Law

While I was working on this chapter, Kent Keller, the minister to singles in the church I serve, came into my study and asked, "Steve, I've been reading Romans 7. Have you read it recently?" I nodded.

"I guess I've read it a hundred times," he continued, "and I never saw what Paul was saying. This is radical stuff. It means that the law is actually dead, and I am now free."

"That's exactly what it says," I agreed. Then I told Kent what I was working on and about my problems teaching freedom with its radical implications. "If I tell people they are really free," I told Kent, "they will think they can do anything they want. I must be very careful because I will be responsible for their disobedience."

Kent smiled. "Steve, you're saying that if you tell people what God says, God can't deal with the implications." (Kent doesn't have any respect for clergy.)

He was right. The problem with most of us in ministry is that we're afraid to proclaim the radical nature of the Christian faith. Our motivations are understandable. We think, *If they accept the truth, they might not obey God—and isn't obedience what the Christian faith is all about?*

Not too long ago, a young man in our church who is studying film making in California was telling another student about his faith in Christ—how Christ had forgiven him and changed his life. His friend stopped him and blurted out, "Hold it right there. I don't want to hear any more. I'm not into rules and guilt."

She missed the whole point! But she can be excused. Most Christians have missed it too. The Christian faith is not about rules and guilt but about freedom: radical, fundamental, exciting, real freedom. There. I've said it again and I'm still glad.

A Lesson in Heresy

Now for a minilesson in heresy. It may seem rather dull, but stay with me because what I'm going to say is important. Heresy—doctrinal deviation from the fundamental truths taught by Scripture and the orthodox Christian church—has historically been a great problem among the people of God. It is a concern, and rightfully so, of faithful leaders of the church through the ages. Scripture says we are to strive to maintain the purity of the faith that was once and for all time revealed to us. (See Jude 3.)

Peter wrote, "But there were also false prophets among the people, even as there will be false teachers among you, who will secretly bring in destructive heresies, even denying the Lord who bought them, and bring on themselves swift destruction. And many will follow their destructive ways, because of whom the way of truth will be blasphemed" (2 Pet. 2:1–2).

Paul wrote to his young friend Timothy, "Now the Spirit expressly says that in latter times some will depart from the faith, giving heed to deceiving spirits and doctrines of demons. . . . Take heed to yourself and to the doctrine. Continue in them, for in doing this you will save both yourself and those who hear you" (1 Tim. 4:1, 16).

So the truth of Scripture is vitally important, and anything which deviates from that truth is heresy. You probably already knew that. But let me tell you something you may not know: almost all heresy is, all things considered, a rather small aberration from biblical Christianity. In other words, heresy is not a total missing of the mark; it is, rather, a missing of the mark in one or two seemingly small areas. Someone has said that Satan will use ninety-nine parts truth to float one lie. That is true and that is usually what happens with heresy.

Heresy has always been a problem in the church. Irenaeus wrote a whole treatise titled *Against the Heresies.* Writing against the second century Gnostics, he condemned what he called godless and impious doctrines.

Clement of Alexandria said that heresies spring from self-conceit, vanity, and deliberate mishandling of Scripture. Tertullian was very hard on philosophers and claimed that they were the fathers of all heresy.

But here is the important thing: Most heresies are right on many doctrines and wrong on only a few. As time passes, those heresies often become totally off base, but they begin with usually a fairly small aberration.

For instance, the heresy of Manichaeism taught that Jesus was a Savior but that He was only one of a number of saviors. Marcionism saw the importance of Christ's person but made a radical break with the Old Testament and the teaching of Judaism. The Nestorian heresy taught that Jesus was divine and human—but juxtaposed those natures as two separate persons in one body. Sometimes there is a very fine line between what is heretical and what is orthodox, biblical Christianity.

That brings me to a particular heresy which pertains to our discussion of freedom: *antinomianism.* Coined by Luther during the Reformation, the word comes from two Greek words—*anti* (meaning "against") and *nomos* (meaning "law"). Thus, *antinomianism* means "against the law."

Martin Luther coined the word when he found that an old friend of his, John Agricola, was teaching that Christians were no longer under any law. Agricola taught that there was no need to keep the Ten Commandments or to obey any moral law whatsoever. The Reformationists, I'm sure you know, taught that we are saved by faith in Christ alone. However, they also taught that once we are saved, we will obey the law. In other words, good works have nothing to do with salvation except that they become a manifestation of it.

Now hear something very important: while the apostle

Paul was not antinomian, *he was very close to it*. Just so, while the Reformation leaders were not antinomian, *they were very close to it*. Also, while the Christian faith is by no means antinomian, *it is very close to it*.

What's the point? Paul would never have had to write a defense of his teaching on freedom if he had not been very close to heresy. Martin Luther would never have had to come back from Wartburg (where he was in hiding) to straighten out the libertarians in Wittenberg if his teaching had not at least implied something close to what they were doing. The Christian faith would not have had to deal with the heresy of antinomianism unless there was something in it which seemed to imply that particular heresy.

That brings me to a syllogism with two premises and a conclusion. Premise: The real Christian faith is close to antinomianism. Premise: A lot of modern day Christianity is not at all close to antinomianism. Conclusion: A lot of modern day Christianity is not real Christianity.

This book is about freedom, and if you don't see the radical nature of the freedom proclaimed in the Bible, you have missed the point, not of the book, but of the Christian faith itself. It's a matter of attitude and mindset. If we start with the belief that Christianity is a religious methodology to make people good or kind or loving, we will end with a set of rules and regulations. And those rules and regulations will continue to widen and broaden until the Christian faith becomes like the Pharisaic religion that Jesus detested. And then Jesus will have died in vain.

The problem with the church is that we have started with the law and ended with disobedience. The thesis of this book is that when you start with freedom you end with obedience. People become antinomian (for the most part) not because they are rebellious or because they don't care but because they are tired. They become antinomian because they just can't keep on keeping on anymore, because they have tried and failed so many times that trying again seems pointless, because the flesh is weak and they can't deal with the guilt anymore.

Becoming antinomian is tragic but not totally ruinous. At least, even though heretical, an antinomian can still be in the camp, hovering near the throne. But people never stop with antinomianism because of a human process every pastor has observed: Law leads to guilt, guilt leads to struggle, struggle leads to failure, failure leads to more guilt, more guilt leads to antinomianism, antinomianism leads to apostasy, and apostasy leads to outright unbelief. Out of that unbelief flow anger and hardness of heart.

It is a tragic process and I have only recently begun to understand. But my new understanding has radically changed the way I deal with people.

Pastors deal with lots of tragedies. Know-it-alls are always telling me they're going to take me out and show me the real world. I've got news for them! I see more of the real world in a week than most people see in a lifetime. I've heard more confessions than a United States attorney at a Watergate trial. I've cleaned up after more suicides, stood before more deathbeds, and buried more babies than I can remember.

But all that is not half as tragic as watching a vibrant, committed Christian slip into the darkness—and not knowing why.

A number of months ago one of the members of the men's Bible study I teach informed me that a mutual friend of ours had become an atheist. I have watched a lot of people take the road to unbelief, but this man had been a faithful pastor and seminary professor. I knew a number of people he had led to Christ. "It's not true!" I raged. "It can't be true! You shouldn't say things like that about him. It's a lie."

Ending the Bible study early, I rushed back to my office and called our friend. "Someone told me this morning that you had become apostate—that you had left the faith and become an atheist. I just want you to know that I called that man a liar. I was right, wasn't I?"

The cold silence on the other end of the line confirmed what I feared, and even as I write my heart is breaking and tears are welling up in my eyes.

I don't know anything that breaks my heart more than seeing someone I love leave the warmth of the fire and slip into the darkness. Every worthy pastor knows what I'm talking about. Over and over, I have tried to make sure that it never happens again. But it keeps happening.

After that incident I started studying the Scriptures without commentaries. Surely in the pure Word of God I would find help! Do you know what I discovered? I discovered that I had been going about it the wrong way. I discovered I had been starting with obedience, instead of where the Bible starts—with freedom. I had been doing the very thing that was causing the problem—that is, I had been attempting to obey the rules, thinking I would find freedom.

Guess what else? I discovered I was walking through the same process as those who had become atheists, and that frightened the living daylights out of me.

I'm not so frightened anymore. Why? Because I have discovered something I had lost in my theology books, a reality that seemed to evade me in my pastoral work. I discovered a glorious truth, so radical I thought it couldn't be true.

But it is.

Do you remember the process I described before? (Law

leads to guilt; guilt leads to struggle; struggle leads to failure; failure leads to more guilt; more guilt leads to antinomianism; antinomianism leads to apostasy; and apostasy leads to anger and hardness of heart.) There is another process, and this process doesn't begin with law, but with freedom and love. Let me share it with you. Love that makes you free leads to guilt. Guilt leads to confession. Confession leads to more forgiveness. Total forgiveness leads to worship. Worship leads to faithfulness.

Do you see it? Faithfulness is the result of a process that begins with love and freedom. Hardness of heart is the result of a process which begins with the law.

I am free! No, I don't mean I am free with a number of ifs, ands, and buts. I mean I am really free. God didn't give me a disclaimer. There was no addendum, no qualifying points from Him. He said, "Steve, you are free." And if you know Him, you are too!

There, I've said it again, and I'm still glad.

CHAPTER 5

BAPTIZED PAGANISM
(Christianity That Isn't)

"And do not be conformed to this world, but be transformed by the renewing of your mind, that you may prove what is that good and acceptable and perfect will of God."

Romans 12:2

Religion is a dangerous thing. It can become an excuse for the violence of human nature. There is no doubt that the people who have conducted the pogroms of history against the Jews were religious people. The medieval Inquisition was a religious movement. Look at Northern Ireland, the Middle East, or South Africa and you will find religion doing service to the violence in humanity. Almost all who fight wars believe they are on God's side.

Religion can become an excuse for intolerance and elitism. Not so long ago the Bible was used to prove that slavery was ordained by God. Religious people have always cited religion as their authority to justify racial prejudice and bigotry. Religion has, more often than most of us would like to admit, been the way religious people separate themselves from the riffraff of humankind. And religious people often divide the world into *us* and *them* to vent the need to be superior.

Religion can also be used as an excuse for a critical spirit. If religion measures the way people act and what they say, then those of us who speak and act properly can correct those who don't. There are people who are perennial fixers of other people's lives. For them, religion is quite convenient.

Religion can also be an excuse for withdrawing from the world. If we are afraid to face reality, religion can create a separate reality for us—one with which we can easily cope. Some religious people have so withdrawn from the world, the flesh and the devil that they are no longer in touch with the hurt and struggle of their fellow human beings—or of themselves. The Bible college which advertised in its catalog that it "was one hundred miles from any known sin" has withdrawn in the name of religion.

Religion can do service in the court of politics. I am always surprised when I find that God is a Republican or a Democrat, a liberal or a conservative. If we can convince ourselves of one of those assertions, politics can be both fun and spiritual.

Religion can be a method for obtaining power. From Constantine to the Holy Roman Emperor to the German Philip of Hesse to Ayatollah Khomeini, people have found religion a convenient way to exercise control over others. In the game of life power is a prized possession, and sometimes the fastest way to get it is in the name of God.

Finally, religion can be a way to achieve wealth. The faithful are always willing to give to anyone who can convince them he or she is acting in God's stead. The trick is getting them to sign the check—easy enough with plenty of God talk.

I could, of course, go on and on. In defense of true religion, however, let me say that atheism and unbelief (consider Stalin and Mao), persecution (such as has happened to the peoples of Romania and Poland), and lack of absolute values (such as the slogan "do your own thing") have slaughtered more people, caused more devastation, and ruined more lives than religion will ever even touch.

Atheists hardly ever build hospitals, start schools, or write symphonies, and long after the pagans have given up their benevolent efforts for the hungry (which had to be emotionally sustained by the musical ditty "We Are the World") the Christians will still be living with and reaching out to the hungry, the dispossessed, and the oppressed—and making a difference. All of the money ever given by pagans to help the world's hurt is mere pittance compared to the money, time, and effort given by believers for hundreds and hundreds of years. Check it out.

THE TRUTH ABOUT RELIGION

The point is this: If we are ever going to be free in the biblical sense of the word, we must distinguish between what people say and what God says. Or to put it another way, organized religion (the institutional functions of human understanding of God and efforts to please Him) and religion in the biblical sense (a relationship of joy, obedience, and worship of the Creator by His creatures) should be understood as two different things. If we aren't able to separate the two, we will remain bound to forms that kill our freedom.

Paul spoke of those who have "a form of godliness but [who deny] its power" (2 Tim. 3:5). Jeremiah spoke his "Thus saith the Lord" against the forms of religion without the meaning:

> For what purpose to Me
> Comes frankincense from Sheba,
> And sweet cane from a far country?
> Your burnt offerings are not acceptable,
> Nor your sacrifices sweet to Me. (Jer. 6:20)

Amos spoke for God too:

> I hate, I despise your feast days,
> And I do not savor your sacred assemblies.

> Though you offer Me burnt offerings and your
>   grain offerings,
> I will not accept them,
> Nor will I regard your fattened peace offerings.
> Take away from Me the noise of your songs,
> For I will not hear the melody of your
>   stringed instruments. (Amos 5:21–23)

Now don't get me wrong. Religion is necessary. I'm not for a moment suggesting that we close down the churches (I do have some rather important vested interest here) or that we junk our liturgies or that we all get a backpack and become flower children again. To the contrary. Outward forms do express inward reality. Because we are social and communicative beings, formal religion will always be a vital part of every culture. The problem comes when the outward forms take the place of the inward reality. It is that confusion from which Jesus redeemed us and for which He died.

Now let me show you two very important areas, in our consideration of human freedom, where religion has gotten confused with reality. They are psychology and culture.

Confusing Psychology with Religion

Have you ever noticed how people seek to express their religious beliefs in a place that is conducive to their psychological disposition? When our psychological disposition is healthy (a very rare situation except for you and me, and sometimes I worry about you), our choice of religious forms is fairly healthy. However, when we have some kind of unhealthy psychological or emotional need, our choice of religious expression can be terribly deceptive. One of the reasons religion is dangerous is that it can become an expression of our own neuroses and sometimes even our psychoses. No matter how crazy you are, how aberrant from the normal, how weird, you can generally find a religious system to express yourself.

While writing this chapter, I was interrupted by one of the church secretaries, who came to report a young man in the lobby of our church administration building shouting at everyone who walked through. I went to find the man, who, for all the world, looked like John the Baptist. He was preaching in our lobby, and he was preaching very loudly.

I asked him what he was doing.

"God has sent me to rebuke your church," he replied.

"That's interesting," I said, thinking of about a dozen possibilities. "What did He send you to rebuke us about?"

"God says you don't care for the poor and the oppressed."

"Maybe you and God got your wires crossed. What do you know about our church?"

"I don't have to know anything about your church. What God told me is enough."

"Listen, buddy," I said with my most authoritarian clergy voice, "you ought to check before you speak. You might be surprised to find out that we are far different than you think. People who are sent by God to rebuke churches and who don't have their facts right, were probably not sent by God."

That is usually enough intimidation to run off all but the most persistent.

But he didn't leave.

I was ready to call the police, but that still small voice said, "What if he is right? What if God has sent him? What if you turn away a true prophet, Steve?" And so, to the horror of the secretaries, I invited him back to my study.

Do you know what I found? A young man who really knew Christ and wanted to serve Him. He had been living on the streets almost four years, and he was venting all his anger and hostility (some of it quite legitimate) at the nearest religious object he could find—our church. At a "Christian" institution in California, he had learned that rebuke was the best way to deal with someone whose doctrine was different from yours or who treated you unfairly. In my study we talked a long time and then we prayed together. We have now met on a number of occasions and I can see, under the angry exterior, a very soft and gentle brother, who desires with all his heart to please Christ. What happened? He was angry and he found a religious form through which he could express his anger.

That happens to all of us; we all can find a religious form to express ourselves. If you like people and enjoy sharing with others, you will probably pick a church with a relational tone to it. If you are, on the other hand, happier with books than with people, you will choose to worship at a church of a more cerebral bent. If you have a fortress mentality you will find a church that makes a clear separation between us and them. If you feel guilty and want to be punished, you might look for a church which confirms your negative self-image. If you are insecure in your religious beliefs, you will probably look for a religious institution in which every doctrine is chiseled in concrete.

We must be very careful not to equate our psychological needs with biblical truth or, to put it another way, we must not universalize our personal psychological proclivity. Let me illustrate.

When I first got serious with God I had come out of a very liberal (just this side of whoopee) graduate school of theology. I thought I was an intellectual, and we intellectuals simply did not stoop to believe in something as obscurantist and silly as the Bible.

Then God came.

I've described the process of my journey from where I was to the Bible thumping fundamentalist I am today in some of my other books. But let me say here it was a long and hard process. The result of the process was not only my intellectual acceptance of the eternal verities of the Christian faith, that process resulted in my becoming quite narrow and opinionated. The psychological wounds I received on the journey (from colleagues who laughed at me, friends who no longer wanted to be my friend, and members of my church who thought I had lost my mind) were wounds which caused some rather shameful character traits with which God had to deal.

During those days I would not allow anyone to disagree with my position without pointing out how silly and superficial their views were. I only attended conferences that confirmed my psychological aberrations. I only read books that fed the flame of my desire to straighten out an apostate church. I was quick to correct everyone I knew. I associated only with those who shared my anger and my hatred of anything that varied with what I knew was the truth.

I'm a lot older now and a little bit wiser. I am learning that my choice of friends, conferences, books, and religious expressions had more to do with my psychological wounds than it did with God. I sometimes think about those days and blush. God, in His love, is now giving me a gentleness and an acceptance I didn't have before. I'm learning to follow Jesus and not my psychological proclivities.

Extreme proclivities are often the focal point of whole religious systems such as Jim Jones' cult. (It causes me to

wince to think that a major religion or theological position affecting all of Christendom could have started because some unwary parents somewhere in history
improperly potty trained their child.)

Well-meaning people often ask me if Christians can
have emotional problems. Of course they can! If you stick
a Christian with a pin, he or she will bleed just as anyone
else bleeds. Christians experience the pain of broken and
poor self-images just as pagans do. Unfortunately, many
Christians become trapped in a theology that causes them
to feel guilty about their pain, so they deny it exists.

That also leads many Christians to churches where they
feel comfortable. Unfortunately, that sometimes means
the church reflects their own neuroses.

Confusing Culture with Religion

Second, there is great danger in confusing cultural
norms with biblical truth. Sometimes the lines between
the two are quite fuzzy.

During the sixties when Jesus people were coming into
the church in droves, I experienced a rude awakening.
These young people, for the most part, had not been
brought up in the traditional church. As they got active in
the church I was serving at the time, I found myself without answers to many of their questions. Why did we do
things the way we did?

One time the young new Jesus Christians herded our
Sunday school children down to the big, old, staid New
England Presbyterian church for a Jesus March. They
marched around shouting "Give me a 'J'; give me an 'E';
give me an 'S'; give me a 'U'; give me an 'S.'" They reminded me of high-school cheerleaders at a football

game. After each letter our children would shout the letter back in unison, all the time marching around the church with "Jesus Loves You" signs.

Now, I don't know about your church, but that kind of demonstration isn't welcome in a New England establishment church. ("It simply isn't done!") When I talked to the young people about it, they answered lovingly, "Pastor, we will respect your authority as our pastor, but could you tell us why we aren't supposed to do it?" Not only did I have no answer but I realized that a lot had passed for Christianity in my ministry that was nothing more than culture. *heritage*

As with psychology, culture often defines doctrine. Culture ought to be determined by theology and doctrine, but that is not often the case.

One time D. L. Moody went to meet Charles Spurgeon at Spurgeon's home in London. Spurgeon had been Moody's hero and, from a distance, his teacher. When Spurgeon answered the door with a cigar in his mouth, Moody practically fell down the stairs in shock. Looking up at Spurgeon, he gasped, "How could you, a man of God, smoke that?"

Spurgeon took the stogie out of his mouth and walked down the stairs to where Moody was still standing in confusion. Putting his index finger on Moody's rather rotund stomach, he smiled. "The same way you, a man of God, could be that fat."

Moody's culture considered smoking a major sin, and Spurgeon's culture considered obesity a major sin. Much to Spurgeon's credit, he pointed it out.

Where am I going with all this? Let me tell you. One of the major reasons Christians are not free is that we have piled layer after layer of psychological and cultural nonsense over our relationship with a person, Jesus Christ. Too often the Christian faith is only a means of baptizing our pagan psychology and culture.

I know. That isn't how it should be, but can we talk? You and I both know it's true. There are magnificent, wonderful exceptions to the rule, such as John Newton, who was wont to say, "Once I was a wild thing on the coast of Africa. But Jesus Christ caught me and tamed me, and now people come to see me the way they come to see the animals in the zoo." Precious few Christians, however, have a clear before-and-after testimony. And we have to look hard to find them. All many people do when they become Christians is become religious.

Neurotic pagans have become neurotic Christians. Fearful pagans have become fearful Christians. Mean pagans have become mean Christians. Critical, judgmental pagans have become critical, judgmental Christians. Bound pagans have become bound Christians. Morally straight pagans have become morally straight Christians. Proper pagans have become proper Christians. Perfectionistic pagans have become perfectionistic Christians.

Do you agree? Not only that, do you agree that it may have happened to you? I won't tell anyone that it's true of you, as long as you don't tell anyone that it's true of me too.

Now, let me tell you the great danger we face. The danger lies in our seeing the problem and trying to "fix" it. May God save us from fixers in the family of God. Inappropriate fixing of symptoms (becoming, with some good old-fashioned willpower and elbow grease, more moral, less critical, and kinder) simply will not do. Our trying to fix the problem only makes matters worse.

Jesus is the only qualified fixer we've got. If we try to

fix a problem with a fix God didn't intend to use to fix our problem, God will give us a problem that even our best efforts at fixing will not fix. "What did you say?" you ask. Let me say it another way: God has ordained a way for us to deal with the problem that culture and psychology inflict on our beliefs, but if we don't do it God's way, the problem will get worse.

The problem is slavery, and the only remedy is the freedom we find in Christ. We are going to talk about that later, but let's look first at some of the inappropriate ways we twist Christianity into something it's not.

TWISTED FAITH: RELIGION MISDEFINED

Many define *religion* as a moral standard. Religion is what makes me good, pure, kind, and compassionate. If that's your definition of religion, then you would do better with a behavioristic psychologist. And if that's how we define religion, we'd better get another one, because the one we have right now isn't working too well.

Have you ever been around Christians who are, from all outward appearances, just about perfect? Well, I have and I don't like them at all. As a matter of fact, when I'm around Christians like that I always feel judged. I want to say, "Why don't you go out and get drunk or something?" I, of course, would never say anything like that . . . but I want to.

I spend a lot of time in my study with people who are as perfect as people can get this side of heaven, and I want to let you in on a secret—most of them are so frightened and hurting that I want to cry for them. They think if they can just get it right, then God will notice and be pleased with them, and they will finally have peace. They are often like the rich man, who thought he would find meaning in his riches only to discover that, as Mark Twain put it, "he had paid too much for his whistle."

Others have defined religion as the focal point of values in a society. In other words, no society can live without shared values, and it is up to religion to provide them. Allan Bloom points out in his very good book *The Closing of the American Mind* the horror of a society without shared values. While Bloom's book is not specifically Christian and, in fact, is in some ways antagonistic to the Christian faith, his analysis of the problems of a society without values is very good.

He wrote rather sarcastically:

Values are insubstantial stuff, existing primarily in the imagination, while death is real. The term "value," meaning the radical subjectivity of all belief about good and evil, serves the easy going quest for comfortable self-preservation.

Value relativism can be taken to be a great release from the perpetual tyranny of good and evil, with their cargo of shame and guilt, and the endless efforts that the pursuit of the one and the avoidance of the other enjoin. . . . One need not feel bad about or uncomfortable with oneself when just a little value adjustment is necessary. . . .

It was not until the sixties that the value insight (i.e., value relativism) began to have its true effects in the United States, as it had had in Germany thirty or forty years earlier. Suddenly a new generation that had not lived off inherited value fat, that had been educated in philosophic and scientific indifference to good and evil, came on the scene . . . and taught their elders a most unpleasant lesson.[5]

Without question, our society desperately needs values; however, though religion does provide values, that is not its primary purpose. When we define the Christian religion only in terms of giving social values, we miss something very important.

Some would define religion in terms of the ritual or liturgy which, when used in public or private worship, draws the participant closer to God. Liturgy (whether informal free church liturgy or the more conventional liturgy of more formal churches) is certainly an important ingredient in religion. In my own private worship I use the liturgy from the Church of Scotland. I tend to grow tired of my own prayers and my own words, and there is something deeply moving about going before the Father in the ancient and meaningful words used throughout the centuries. However, if that becomes my definition of the Christian religion, it can become quite empty and void of meaning.

Some would define religion as doctrine. I belong to a branch of Christendom where doctrine is extremely important, and I would not lessen that importance. Throughout history those who knew the truth and could define it in a doctrinal way were the ones who stood against tyranny and persecution. When the going gets tough, the tough get going. And those who are tough cling to a truth that lasts long after feelings and emotional worship have dissipated.

Oswald Chambers once said, "The way our heart is hardened is by sticking to our convictions instead of to Christ." He's right. One can be doctrinally pure and still be very much outside the kingdom. Scripture tells us that even the demons believe right doctrine (James 2:19). Acceptance of biblical doctrinal truths is important, but that certainly must not define the Christian religion.

Still others define religion as something that makes them feel good. God is a big Santa in the sky whose primary reason for existence is to give them what they want, what makes them happy. Truth isn't important because truth is what works for you.

A friend of mine recently saw one of those bumper stickers which read, "If It Feels Good, Do It." He told me he thought about ramming that car and saying when the driver dared to question him, "It felt good. I did it."

Of course, some aspects of religion do make one feel better about oneself. As a matter of fact, people who are religious generally live longer than those who aren't. Study after study has produced clear evidence that belief in and worship of God is psychologically healthy. But we dare not define Christianity in those terms. That would be putting the cart before the horse—believing that the Christian faith works and is therefore true, rather than understanding that it works because it is true.

Some would define religion in terms of ethnic or cultural conformity. There are, of course, ethnic churches which minister primarily to immigrants from other nations. They conduct services in the native language of the home country and reinforce the ethnic and national roots of their worshipers.

Yet cultural conformity occurs in all places of worship to one degree or another. A Southern Baptist church differs from an Anglican church because, sociologically speaking, the makeup of the churches is different. Certain things are acceptable in a Southern Baptist church and other things are not. That's true of the Anglican church too. And what constitutes acceptable and unacceptable behavior would probably differ significantly between the two churches.

I believe it was Os Guinness who, during the Jesus movement, talked about how grandparents related to the Jesus People of the Sixties. The grandparents knew God,

and their lives and values were determined by that knowledge. Their children came along and watched their parents pray and worship. It seemed a reasonable thing to do,
so they prayed and worshiped in the same way. But they
had never known God—only the forms by which their
parents had expressed that knowledge. Then the young
people of the sixties, the grandchildren, came along and
asked their parents a lot of questions: "Why shouldn't I
sleep with my boyfriend? Why is it wrong to smoke pot?
Why must I live by your rules?" The parents generally
answered, "Just because." They just didn't have any other
answer.

Those young people saw their parents as hypocrites. To
them the church held to values that had no meaning. They
were angry and, by the way, they were also right. Then
they went out and did their own thing. It caused more
tragedy and heartbreak than anyone could have imagined.
That generation, doing it their way, had one of the highest
suicide rates in history. Their parents were doing the right
thing for the wrong reason and, because it was the right
thing, were reasonably happy. Their children saw only the
hypocrisy, so they did the wrong things for the right reasons and were miserable.

Then came the Jesus Movement with thousands upon
thousands of young people finding Christ. Their parents
were horrified. One mother was reported in *Look* magazine to have said that she would rather have had her
daughter smoke pot than participate in the movement.
"At least," the mother said, "I can understand that."

Then an amazing thing happened. The young people
came into the church and began to relate to the older people their grandparents' age, not to church members who
were their parents' age. The young people and old people
shared a secret that the middle generation didn't under-

stand: They understood values, and they understood and knew the source of those values.

One can go to church and pray and live by certain moral standards (and serve as an officer of the church and wear the right clothes to services and use the right language) simply because it is the proper thing to do. As Corrie Ten Boom said, "Sleeping in a garage doesn't make you a car."

I could, of course, continue with this list. The point is that when religion is defined in any other way than Jesus defined it, any religion will do.

The important thing is that we go back to our roots and find out what this life is all about. Turn the page and that's exactly what we'll do.

Part Two

JESUS AND THE TRUTH ABOUT FREEDOM

CHAPTER 6

BACK TO THE BASICS
(Getting Started Right)

*"For as by one man's disobedience many were made
sinners, so also by one Man's obedience many will be
made righteous. Moreover the law entered that the
offense might abound. But where sin abounded, grace
abounded much more, so that as sin reigned in death,
even so grace might reign through righteousness to
eternal life through Jesus Christ our Lord."*
Romans 5:19–21

When a football team begins to lose an undue number of games, the members go back to practicing the basics. If the basics aren't right, the team certainly can't pull off any fancy stuff!

I taught swimming and diving for a number of years, and I especially remember one young boy named Billy. Billy had watched so many professional divers and wanted so much to dive like them that he refused to take time to learn the basics. Time after time I tried to help Billy see that the most important thing about diving was to keep his head in the proper position. If his head entered the water properly, I explained, the rest of his body would enter the water properly—at least, more properly than it had been.

Billy would dive into the pool, do a belly flop, and come up grinning. "Mr. Brown," he would shout, "were my feet together?"

"Billy, I don't care whether your feet were together or not. Make sure your head is straight, then everything else will work out."

The next time Billy would stand on the edge of the pool and really concentrate. Then he would dive and, once again, make a mess of it. "Mr. Brown, were my hands together?"

"Billy," I would groan in frustration, "I'm going to get you a neck brace and weld it onto your head. For the hundredth time, if your head is right the rest of you will be right. If your head is wrong, the rest of you will be wrong."

It's the same way with the Christian faith. If we get the basics right, there's a fair chance we'll get the rest of it right too.

So let's talk basics.

DEFINING THE TERMS

First, let's define some terms. This may seem redundant if you've been a Christian very long, but it might help the newcomers to our family.

The first term is *justification*. Justice carries strong connotations. It means to set things right or to balance the books. Justification is the process whereby we are made right. In Christianity, justification by faith alone is a biblical doctrine which teaches that when we come to Christ, we are reconciled to God and made right in His eyes by the sacrifice of Christ alone.

Have you heard the story of the judge whose son was brought before him for drunken driving? The judge, sworn to uphold justice, fined his son heavily. But then he stepped down off the bench and paid the fine himself. That's what the Father has done for us! God has paid our fine—balanced the books, if you will—by sending His Son to pay our penalty on the cross.

The second term we will be working with is *sanctification*. It comes from a word meaning to make holy or to be set apart for a special purpose. In the Christian sense, it means the process whereby a Christian is set apart unto God, becoming more and more like Christ.

When you became a Christian, you were set apart in a special way as God's own. Peter said, "But you are a chosen generation, a royal priesthood, a holy nation, His own special people" (1 Pet. 2:9). In a sense you are sanctified by the very fact that you are a Christian, but you grow in holiness and sanctification. Becoming like Christ is a process John Wesley called "moving on to perfection."

The third term is *grace*. Grace, someone has said, is not a blue-eyed blonde. Grace is God's totally unmerited favor toward the believer.

A father caught his son smoking. "You know my displeasure in you right now," he admonished him. "I've always told you I would punish you severely if I ever caught you smoking. You deserve three smacks across your bottom with my belt."

Thereupon, the father got his belt, but he hit the boy only once. Then he sent his son up to his room.

A short time later, the father climbed the stairs to his son's room and asked, "Would you like to go out and get some ice cream?" Sitting at the ice cream parlor, the father said, "You do know that when I caught you smoking you deserved three hits with my belt?"

"Yes, sir."

"You noticed that you only got one, didn't you?"

"Yes, sir."

"Son, that is mercy, and I want you to remember the lesson. Are you enjoying your ice cream?"

"Yes, sir."

"Son, the ice cream is grace. Remember that too."

THE GOOD NEWS

Now let's continue with our discussion of basics. In a previous chapter I talked about how the real Christian faith is very close to heresy. Let me quote extensively from

D. M. Lloyd-Jones's commentary on Romans 6:1 where Paul says, "What shall we say then? Shall we continue in sin that grace may abound?"

There is a sense in which the doctrine of justification by faith only is a very dangerous doctrine; dangerous, I mean, in the sense that it can be misunderstood. It exposes a man to this particular charge. People listening to it may say, "Ah, there is a man who does not encourage us to live a good life, he seems to say that there is no value in our works, he says that 'all our righteousness are as filthy rags'. . . . Therefore what he is saying is that it does not matter what you do, sin as much as you like." . . . There is thus clearly a sense in which the message of "justification by faith only" can be dangerous, and likewise with the message that salvation is entirely of grace. . . . I say therefore that if our preaching does not expose us to that charge and to that misunderstanding, it is because we are not really preaching the gospel. Nobody has ever brought this charge against the Church of Rome, but it was brought frequently against Martin Luther; indeed that was precisely what the Church of Rome said about the preaching of Martin Luther. They said, "This man who was a priest has changed the doctrine in order to justify his own marriage and his own lust", . . . and so on. "This man", they said, "is an antinomian; and that is heresy." That is the very charge they brought against him. It was also brought against George Whitefield two hundred years ago. It is the charge that formal dead Christianity—if there is such a thing—has always brought against this startling, staggering message, that God "justifies the ungodly", and that we are saved, not by anything we do, but in spite of it, entirely and only by the grace of God through our Lord and Saviour Jesus Christ.

That is my comment; and it is a very important comment for preachers. I would say to all preachers: If your preaching of salvation has not been misunderstood in that way, then you had better examine your sermons again, and you had better make sure that you really are preaching the salvation that is offered in the New Testament to the ungodly, to the sinner, to those who are dead in trespasses and sins, to those who are enemies of God. There is this kind of dangerous element about the true presentation of the doctrine of salvation.[6]

When we talk about the basics of the Christian faith we are talking about something very dangerous—the basic good news of Christ's coming into the world.

Let me tell you a true story.

There once was a king who loved being king. He liked sitting on the throne and making decisions; he liked living in the castle; he liked the symbolic functions of his office; he liked visiting the towns and villages of the kingdom and meeting his subjects; he liked the authority and power because he could use them to help his people.

Not only did the king like being king, but his people throughout the kingdom praised him for ruling so benevolently and wisely. The people knew they could trust their king to do the right thing for them and for the kingdom, and they were right. Because of the king's wisdom, the kingdom was prosperous and peaceful.

When the king's son was born, the people put on a great celebration. Now there was an heir! The people knew the king would be a good father and that his son would some day be as great and wise as his father.

The king loved his son more than his own life. His greatest joy was to spend time with his son. Each evening after the day's duties were accomplished, the king would go out into the formal gardens behind the castle and play with his son. The thought of those times with his son often made the hard task of ruling a little easier. Sometimes when he faced a difficult decision or had to settle a dispute or complete a project, the king would think, "When this is over, I can be with my son," and he would smile.

One day the king's son got lost. It was one of the most tragic days that had ever passed in the kingdom. He didn't mean to get lost. He loved his father as much as his father loved him, and those times in the evening with his father were the happiest times of his young life.

But one day his father had a particularly busy day and was late for their daily meeting in the castle gardens. So the boy decided to explore. There was certainly nothing wrong with that, except this boy was very little and very young, and nobody had told him how easy it is for a little boy to get lost.

It happened before the boy knew it. He was just walking and thinking about his father when, looking up, he found himself in the forest behind the castle. Nothing looked familiar! At first he was calm because his father would come soon and find him, but, as he waited, he began to panic. Then he began to run away from the castle. His clothes caught on broken limbs and tore. A couple of times he fell in mud holes, and once he cut himself on a jagged rock.

Eventually the little boy wandered into one of the villages of the kingdom. To be perfectly honest, by that time he looked more like a little beggar than a prince. The little boy would go up behind someone, grab his coat, pull on it and say, "Mister, I'm the king's son. Would you help me get home?"

"Sure you are, kid," the man would laugh, "and I'm his wife."

"But you don't understand," the little boy would say to another. "I got lost, and I can't find my father."

Most folks simply ignored the little boy, and those who didn't ignore him laughed at him. Pretty soon the little boy was forced to beg for pennies just so he could buy bread to keep from starving.

Meanwhile, back at the castle, the king spent a sleepless night looking for his son. He looked everywhere he knew to look, but the boy was nowhere to be found. By morning the king suspected that someone had kidnapped his son and feared that he would never see the boy again.

The king called all his armies together, told them what had happened, and sent them into the kingdom looking for his son. He offered great rewards to anyone who could give him information leading to the discovery of his son. But to the king's great sorrow, the little boy was not found.

Hours blended into days, days into weeks, weeks into months, and months into years. The little boy was no longer a little boy; he had grown into a strong young man.

At first he really had thought he was the king's son, but so many adults had told him differently that he began to think maybe it had been a dream. After all, adults knew those kinds of things. As the years passed he forgot about the castle and about his heritage. It didn't take so many years to forget about the dream altogether.

Then the young man began to run with the wrong crowd. Murder, stealing, rape—nothing was beneath them. But he was still a prince. If you are a prince (even when you don't know it), it shows. Eventually the young man became the leader of the gang. He surpassed all of his friends in his unlawful acts and spurred them on to even greater acts of lawlessness. Years after he had left the castle and his father, the king's son had become the most wanted criminal in the kingdom.

Then one day, through a rather complicated set of circumstances (too complicated to detail here), the king found out that his own son was the kingdom's most wanted criminal. At first he couldn't believe it, but the more he checked, the more it became clear that he had found his beloved son, and in finding him, the king faced a terrible dilemma.

The king loved his son, but he was also fair and just. He knew if he released his own son who had committed terrible crimes, he would need to release all the others who had committed crimes. That was unacceptable.

And so the king's son was arrested and brought before a judge who condemned him to be executed for his crimes. The verdict was just. The king's son was thrown in a dungeon beneath the castle where he had once lived to wait for his execution.

On the night before the young man was to die, the king made his way to the prison beneath the castle. Opening his son's cell, he walked in and sat on the bunk across from his son. The king sat there a long time looking at his son before he spoke.

"You are my son. Did you know that?"

"Someone told me."

"Have you ever wondered, over these years, about your parents?"

"Sometimes, but I had a good life, and it wasn't that important."

"Well, I have never stopped wondering about you— where you were and what had become of you. You have never been out of my mind and heart.

"My son," the king continued, his voice trembling with emotion and the tears running down the age lines in his face, "I loved you with a great love, but you became lost. I did everything I knew to do. I sent out my soldiers; I offered a great reward; I have never ceased to search for you. But now it has come to this and tomorrow you are to die.

"But, son, I have decided to allow you to go free."

With those words, the old king got up and walked out of his son's cell into the crisp night air.

The young man went over to the cell door and tested it. *Well, what do you know?* he thought to himself, *that old man left it open.*

The king's son grabbed his coat, threw it over his shoulder, and with a cynical smile spoke aloud: "That stupid, old man! He thinks because he has set me free I will come back to his castle and be his lackey. Well, he is more senile than I thought." And with that the young man disappeared up the stairs into the night air.

Some two weeks later the king's son found out what price his freedom had cost. On the day of his scheduled execution, the requirements of the law had been met. His own father had taken his place before the executioner and had literally died that he might be free. It was sobering news.

You probably have some questions: What did the son do? Did he return to the castle and become king? Did he accept his heritage? Did he even care about the price his father had paid for his freedom? Did he decide to obey the law?

I'm not sure because, you see, you are the son and I am the son.

Scripture says, "For when we were still without strength, in due time Christ died for the ungodly. For scarcely for a righteous man will one die; yet perhaps for a good man someone would even dare to die. But God demonstrates His own love toward us, in that while we were still sinners, Christ died for us" (Rom. 5:6–8).

MORE GOOD NEWS

When you became a Christian (if you have) you realized that a great price has been paid for you—that Christ died on a cross for your sins, and that you are now justified before God. At that moment you moved into a new relationship with God. No longer are you just His creature— you are now His child and a part of His family.

"There is therefore now no condemnation to those who are in Christ Jesus, who do not walk according to the flesh, but according to the Spirit. For the law of the Spirit of life in Christ Jesus has made me free from the law of sin and death. For what the law could not do in that it was weak through the flesh, God did by sending His own Son in the likeness of sinful flesh, on account of sin: He condemned sin in the flesh, that the righteous requirement of the law might be fulfilled in us who do not walk according to the flesh but according to the Spirit" (Rom. 8:1–4).

That's all basic. Let me tell you something else that's basic: When God is your Father, He never stops being your Father. To put it in theological language, not only is your justification (being saved) by grace, your sanctification (becoming more like Christ) is by grace too.

The trouble is that most Christians think they're saved by grace but grow by sweat. Many of us believe that when we were saved, God took our slate filled with sin and rebellion and wiped it clean. That's a lie and it comes from the pit of hell.

Listen! God took our slate and He broke it in pieces and threw it away. He does not deal with his family by keeping track on a slate of how we are doing. The slate is irrelevant because of the blood of Christ.

I'm sure you've heard the story about the farmer who had just gotten married at the country church. He and his new wife, still dressed in her wedding gown, were driving away from the church in his horse-drawn wagon. About a mile down the road, the horse stumbled. Pulling over to the side of the road, the farmer got off the wagon, walked in front of the horse, looked the horse in the eye, and said, "That's one."

A short time later the horse stumbled again. The new bride watched, puzzled, as the farmer once again pulled over to the side of the road, got out of the wagon, walked to the front of the horse, looked the horse in the eye, and warned, "That's two."

They had gone no more than a half mile further when the horse stumbled once again. The farmer reached behind the wagon seat for his shotgun, climbed down, walked to the front, and shot the horse.

"What did you do that for?" shouted his new wife. "All the horse did was stumble."

The farmer took his seat in the wagon, looked at his new wife, and said, "That's one!"

We don't admit it, but that's how we feel God deals with us, and it has become the great tragedy in the church.

The word *gospel* means "good news." If the good news applies only to my becoming a part of the family of God, and not to my staying there, then it is no longer good news. If I couldn't be good enough to get into the kingdom before I was a Christian, what in the world makes me think I can be good enough to stay there?

A friend of mine, just before she turned away from her year-old Christian faith, told me, "Pastor, I just can't deal with this any more. I had a problem with guilt and self image before I became a Christian. Now the problem has doubled and it's getting worse every day. I don't think I'm turning away from Christ. I will have to think about that and get some issues straight in my mind to be sure, but I do know I can't be with Christians any more. It isn't a matter of my happiness. It's a matter of my survival!"

What happened to my friend? Something was seriously, horribly wrong. In my heart I wanted to help her, but because I knew and loved her, I knew she was pointing to a reality in the family of Christ that had devastated her. I didn't tell her to get back into fellowship with other Christians. (I didn't tell her not to either.) I just listened and told her that someday she would come back to the family and their wholeness would help her. I have prayed a lot that what I told her could be true.

Stephen Donaldson has a delightful series of books (two trilogies) called *The Thomas Covenant Chronicles* which tell the story of Thomas Covenant and his efforts to heal the wounded Land, a realm of magic and peril, where he fights a bitter battle against sin and madness personified by Lord Foul. Book two of the second trilogy tells of Covenant's friend, Linden Avery, a doctor who was unwittingly drawn to the Land with Covenant. Linden is especially sensitive to the Land and to Thomas Covenant, who had become wounded previously.

> Then with a shock of recognition she saw that the wound was more than a knife-thrust in his chest: it was a stab to the very heart of the Land. The hole had become a pit before her, and its edge was a sodden hillside, and the blood spewing over her was the life of the Earth. The Land was bleeding to death. Before she could even cry out, she was swept away across the murdered body of the ground.[7]

A man gave our church a wonderful compliment a few weeks ago. He came up to me and said, "Pastor, you don't know me but I have been attending this church for almost six months. I always sat on the back row and just listened. I had been so wounded by my last church that I simply didn't have whatever it takes to get involved in another one. So I just sat. I listened to the teaching and the laughter and, gradually, my wounds started healing. Your church is a place of healing, and I wanted to thank you."

That's what the church is all about. We live, to use Donaldson's words, in a "wounded land." The horror is that the church, God's land, isn't a whole lot different. By our narrow, unloving, critical, and unforgiving spirits, we have closed the door on those who have no other place to go. Every time God's people have gotten away from the healing medicine of grace we have hurt the land God cultivated and created for His own.

CHAPTER 7

IT'S THE LAW

(God's Gateway to Freedom)

"Oh, how I love Your law!
It is my meditation all the day."
Psalm 119:97

If you don't have some serious questions right now, then you haven't properly read the preceding chapters. In fact, when Christians don't have some questions, they probably believe something other than the Christian faith.

Biblical theology is sometimes like trying to pack a suitcase with too many clothes. Every time you think you've got it packed, you look and something is sticking out. So you open the suitcase, tuck the shirt back in, and close it once more—only to find something else sticking out.

I'm a Five-Point Calvinist. That means that I accept a certain theological way of looking at things. To be perfectly honest, I believe my theological position is correct. (If I didn't, I would believe something else.) But the problem with identifying with a particular theological position is that everyone who doesn't hold to that particular theological position will point to the items sticking out of your suitcase.

The problem with all of us who are Bible believers and who hold particular views is that something always sticks out of the suitcase. Do you know why? Because God doesn't fit in any of our systems. He is bigger than everything we have ever thought, written, or imagined.

Calvin called the Bible "God's baby talk." By that he didn't mean that the Bible wasn't true but that an infinite God, in order to communicate with finite beings, must keep the fodder down low where we can get to it.

When the subject is freedom, some questions are only natural. Not all of the questions can be resolved, and I suspect that when you finish reading this book you will be able to point to some things that are sticking out of the suitcase. However, sometimes something seems to be sticking out of the suitcase when it really isn't. The law is one of those things. Law and freedom simply don't appear to go together in the same Christian suitcase. But when we really listen to what the Bible is saying, we begin to understand the balance and wonder of God's revelation of truth.

The Bible is filled with clear admonishments about morality, ethics, and the law. Over and over again we are told how we should act, what we should say, and what we should think. Not only that, some very harsh things are said about those who ignore the law, who turn away from God and disregard God's standards.

How does that compare with what I have said up to this point about freedom? How can we be free and obedient at the same time? If we are called to be servants, how can we still be free? Isn't the idea of freedom, in the sense I am using it, a pagan or New Age idea? Doesn't the Christian idea of freedom connote only freedom from sin? Isn't freedom just another name for obedience?

Those questions, it seems to me, can be summed up in one: How does freedom relate to God's law?

It's a good question, and I want to deal with it biblically and thoroughly before we finish. Let's start with Jesus. (Not a bad place to begin.)

THE PURPOSE OF THE LAW

Evidently Jesus had been criticized or had anticipated some criticism about His teaching regarding law and freedom. Speaking to the issue that had been (or would be) raised He said, "Do not think that I came to destroy the Law or the Prophets. I did not come to destroy but to fulfill. For assuredly, I say to you, till heaven and earth pass away, one jot or one tittle will by no means pass from the law till all is fulfilled. Whoever therefore breaks one of the least of these commandments, and teaches men so, shall be called least in the kingdom of heaven; but whoever does and teaches them, he shall be called great in the kingdom of heaven" (Matt. 5:17–19).

Before we look at what the Bible says is the purpose of the law, let's look at some of the interesting points in that text.

First, please note that unless Jesus was giving the impression that He was going to destroy the law, He would never have spoken these words. If Jesus had said nothing to imply that He was going to destroy the law, He would never have needed to address the issue.

In chapter four we saw how Paul had the same problem. If he had not been saying something very close to antinomianism, he would never have written the letter to the Galatians. Similarly, if Jesus had not said something very close to suggesting that the law should be destroyed, He would never have had to say anything about the subject at all.

A well-known Christian lecturer was speaking at a conference in California where he had spoken two or three years before. After his first lecture a man came up to him and said, "I want to check something with you. I've been quoting you ever since you were here the first time, and I wanted to make sure I was quoting you properly. You did say last time that if someone is committing adultery they ought to cut back some?"

The speaker was horrified. If it had been me, I would

have gone back to my notes of the first conference and pored over them trying to find what it was that caused that man to so miss what I had said.

I don't know if this speaker defended himself or tried to correct the man's first impression, but I would have said, "Some of you think that, last time I was here, I was trying to destroy the law that forbids adultery. That simply isn't true. I was not trying to destroy it; I was trying to fulfill it. I was trying to say that God forgives you and that the best way to stop any sin is to know that you are forgiven."

And so Jesus was, of course, not trying to destroy the law. He may have been afraid that this was the impression people were getting. But nothing could have been further from the truth. He was not destroying the law, but—and here is the important point—He was saying something that could be taken that way.

Now the question before the house is this: If everything I said in the previous chapters is true, why the law? In other words, if we are really free, why even bother with the law? Obviously the law is important, or Jesus would have destroyed it.

I move the previous question: What is the purpose of the law?

The Parameters of God's Desire

First, the law reflects the mind of God. If you want to know what God thinks about adultery or stealing or dishonesty or a variety of other kinds of behavior, check out His clear direction in the law. The Ten Commandments are not called the ten suggestions. All of the teaching in the Bible about morality, ethics, and Christian behavior was given so that we might know exactly how God feels on those particular subjects.

You are near, O LORD,
And all Your commandments are truth.
Concerning Your testimonies,
I have known of old that You have founded them
    forever. (Ps. 119:151–152)

Here is the point: The law reflects the parameters of
God's desire—*not the parameters of His love.* When those
two get confused, then the law is used improperly.

Parents often ask me what they should do about their
adult children's unacceptable behavior. For instance, a
parent will ask, "My son has just told us that he is a homosexual. How should we react?" Or, "My daughter is
living with a man and she says that they may or may not
get married. How should I deal with it?" Or "My boy
drinks like a fish and cusses like a sailor. What should I
do?"

In each case, I tell parents to clarify their standards and
to refuse to participate in any action which requires them
to compromise those standards (for instance, allowing
their daughter or son's live-in friend to stay in the parents'
house, affirming the sexual lifestyle of the homosexual
son or daughter). However, I always recommend separat-
ing the standard of behavior from the reality of love. In
other words, never stop loving even if you stop approv-
ing.

Do you know where I got that? I got it from Jesus. Do
you remember when the woman was caught in adultery?
The religious leaders were going to stone her and Jesus
said that only those who had no sin were allowed to
throw stones. They all decided to quietly go away. John
wrote: "When Jesus had raised Himself up and saw no
one but the woman, He said to her, 'Woman, where are
those accusers of yours? Has no one condemned you?' She
said, 'No one, Lord.' And Jesus said to her, 'Neither do I

condemn you; go and sin no more'" (John 8:10–11).

In Matthew 23:37, Jesus is standing on a hill, overlooking the city of Jerusalem. His words are filled with pathos: "O Jerusalem, Jerusalem, the one who kills the prophets and stones those who are sent to her! How often I wanted to gather your children together, as a hen gathers her chicks under her wings, but you were not willing!" Do you see it? It was not the horror of what Jerusalem had done which prevented Jesus from loving and accepting them. It was their own unwillingness to let Him love them.

The message of Jesus is clear: "'Those who are well have no need of a physician, but those who are sick. But go and learn what this means, "I desire mercy and not sacrifice," For I did not come to call the righteous, but sinners, to repentance'" (Matt. 9:12–13). Jesus didn't always approve of behavior but He kept on loving. We are called to do the same.

A Measure

Second, the law functions as a measure by which believers can determine their progress. "For the righteous God tests the hearts and minds" (Ps. 7:9). "You have tested my heart; You have visited me in the night; You have tried me and have found nothing; I have purposed that my mouth shall not transgress" (Ps. 17:3).

Now it is important to know that any testing of our walk with God isn't for His benefit. Too many of us think God sits in the heavens dreaming of ways He can test us to see how we are doing. He looks down and says to His angels, "Look at that! I had such high hopes for him. I really thought he would do better than that." Of course not! Testing has to do with us, not God. He already knows how we are doing.

In college I had an English professor who gave a lot of tests but never graded them. He said, after our class finished the first test, "Now some of you have done very well on this test, and some of you have done horribly. I'm not a teacher who gets his kicks from finding out which you are. But if you are any kind of student at all, you are interested in how you did. So, here are the answers, and I want you to go over your own test and grade it."

Of course, we figured he was checking on our honesty and that he would ask us to turn in the test. You can imagine how surprised we were when he then said, "I don't want to see your tests. The only important thing is that you know how you did. In a few years I probably won't even remember your name. Then your enjoyment of English literature will be based on how much you absorbed in this class. This test is for you, not for me."

Well, that's what the law does for us. It's an exam that God doesn't grade. (The grade was already accomplished on the cross by Jesus, and it was an "A.") You are the one for whom the test was designed. Check out God's will as expressed in Scripture and you will know how far you have come (for encouragement), how much you have failed (for confession), and how far you have to go (for trust).

A Teacher

Third, the law is our teacher, bringing us to Christ and keeping us there. Paul wrote to the Galatians: "Therefore the law was our tutor to bring us to Christ, that we might be justified by faith" (3:24). He wrote to the Romans,

"What shall we say then? Is the law sin? Certainly not! On the contrary, I would not have known sin except through the law. For I would not have known covetousness unless the law had said, 'You shall not covet'" (7:7).

And so the law of God allows me to see my failure. If I hadn't known about my failure, I would never have come to Christ. And every time I go to the law to check how I am doing, those areas where I have not been faithful to the law cause me to turn anew to Christ for forgiveness, acceptance, and strength.

Did you know that the Christian church is the only organization in the world where the only qualification for membership is that you are not qualified? Not only that, properly understood, the Christian church is the only organization in the world where the only qualification for maintaining your membership is not being qualified to maintain your membership.

Do you ever wonder why Christ spent so much time with prostitutes and sinners? He said, "Those who are well have no need of a physician, but those who are sick" (Matt. 9:12). In other words, Jesus is a doctor, and His business is helping sick people become whole. If you aren't sick, or if you don't think you are sick, He won't appeal to you. The problem with the religious people of Jesus' day was that they were as sick as the prostitutes and sinners, but they didn't know it.

I have a friend who is a judge. He isn't a Christian and he doesn't understand why I am. But we are still friends. When I was in his town a number of years ago, I called him up and suggested that we get together.

"I meet my friends in bars," he laughed.

"You name the bar," I countered, much to his surprise, "and I'll meet you there."

That evening when I got to the bar, I found that he had

come with a prostitute. (I suspect he was playing a game called "Shock the Reverend." One of these days I'm going to do something very unclergylike and play a game called "Shock the Layman.") I pretended not to be surprised, and, as a matter of fact, I wasn't much. When his escort went to the ladies' room, he turned to me and pointed to the people standing along the bar. "Steve, all those people are sick." I suspect I raised my eyebrows.

"Don't get me wrong," he added hastily. "I'm sick, too. The only difference is that I know it and they don't."

He was not far from the kingdom. Jesus loves people like my friend. He loves people who know they are sick.

How do we know we are sick? We check the law. How do we know we need Him? Check the law. The business of the law is to drive us to the Physician.

A Road Map

And fourth, the law informs us where the mine fields are.

> Oh, how I love Your law!
> It is my meditation all the day.
> You, through Your commandments, make me
>   wiser than my enemies. (Ps. 119:97–98)

Most people, if they were honest, would admit that they define sin in terms of enjoyment. In other words, if you didn't enjoy it, it wasn't a sin. Conversely, if you did enjoy it, it probably was. By defining sin that way, we make God into a deity whose main purpose is to keep us from enjoying ourselves. A friend of mine says that everything she likes is either fattening, bad for her, or a sin.

Balderdash!

That simply isn't true. Instead, the law tells us how to

be the happiest and the most fulfilled in a fallen world where things are never going to be right. If you want to live in this kind of world as skillfully and successfully as possible, obey the law of God. Some call me a cynic (I say realist) because I believe the main business of life is to get between two hospitals without messing it up too bad. I believe we are born in one hospital and die in another, and the object of life is to get from one to the other as successfully as possible. The way to do that is to pay very close attention to the law.

Someone told me about a priest who said when he was young, "I want to win the world to Christ." In his forties he said, "I would like to win as many as possible to Christ." In his sixties, he prayed, "Lord, don't let me lose too many."

I can identify with that. Maybe it's my basic cynicism, but, whatever it is, I feel the best thing I can do in my life is to be as obedient to God as possible. I don't feel that way because I am such a wonderful person but because the world is such a mess that I need a guide. It's a mine field and I don't want to step on the mines. I've got enough troubles already.

The reason the Jews see "Holy Torah" as the greatest gift God has given them is because they have a secret: they have a road map that shows them how the world works. The law is your road map too. It helps us find our way around the strange country of life. Without it we can get terribly hurt and lost.

You see, when God says not to commit adultery, He isn't trying to keep us from having fun. He tells us not to commit adultery because He doesn't want us to get hurt. He commands us to love our neighbor, not because He wants to keep us busy but because that's the best way to live with our neighbor.

WARNING: THE LAW CAN DESTROY

Now it is inappropriate to use the law for any reason other than the four above. But, far more than being inappropriate and unbiblical, it is destructive to the Body of Christ. Paul said, "The letter kills, but the Spirit gives life" (2 Cor. 3:6).

Now let's examine some inappropriate uses of the law.

The Law Doesn't Save

First, it is inappropriate to use the law as a means of getting to God. In a previous chapter we saw that salvation is by faith in Christ alone. If you add anything to that, then you have missed the whole point.

Before the Reformation Martin Luther was in his monk's cell weeping because of his sins. His confessor, a young man, simply didn't know what to do, so he began repeating the Apostles' Creed.

"I believe in God the Father Almighty, Maker of heaven and earth; And in Jesus Christ His only Son our Lord; who was conceived by the Holy Ghost, born of the Virgin Mary, suffered under Pontius Pilate, was crucified, dead, and buried; He descended into hell; the third day He rose again from the dead; He ascended into heaven, and sitteth on the right hand of God the Father Almighty; From thence He shall come to judge the quick and the dead.

"I believe in the Holy Ghost; the holy Catholic Church; the communion of Saints; the forgiveness of sins; the. . . ."

"Wait!" Luther interrupted his confessor. "What did you say?"

"What do you mean, what did I say?"

"That last part. What was it again?"

"Oh, that. I said, 'I believe in the forgiveness of sins.'"

"The forgiveness of sins," Luther said as if savoring each word. "The forgiveness of sins. Then there is hope for me somewhere. Then maybe there is a way to God."[8]

That, of course, was the beginning of the Reformation. Martin Luther realized that he was not good and that depending on his goodness to get him to God would get him in terrible trouble. So if anyone tells you to put your trust in Christ and then adds anything to that—baptism, goodness, obedience, love, belief in the Bible, going to church—then they are lying to you. "But as many as received [put their trust in] Him, to them He gave the right to become children of God, to those who believe in His name" (John 1:12).

The Law Doesn't Sanctify

Second, it is inappropriate to use the law as a means of staying close to God. Most of us know this in our minds but have trouble really believing it with our hearts.

Most of us play a game (I'll bet you do too) called "if you do something bad, do something good to balance the books." It's like dieting—if you eat a piece of cake, you have to go without something important later on to get those pounds off.

Listen, your goodness does not bring you to God, and it will not keep you there either! Of course, godliness flows from a vital relationship with Christ, but godliness does not keep you in that relationship.

An unfortunate and popular teaching today suggests that if you don't live a holy life, if you don't manifest righteousness, then you could not possibly belong to Christ. I understand that kind of teaching and have taught it myself. But I was wrong. (It was only the second time in my life I was ever wrong. The first was one time when I thought I was wrong.)

Not only was I wrong, but what I taught was dangerous. I had done something I had no right to do: I had told some of God's people that they weren't God's people. Nobody except God has the right to say that.

Most of the time our relationship with Christ is manifested by our walking with Him in holiness. But what of those times when we don't walk in holiness? What about the times we have known God's will and have done just the opposite, when we belonged to Him but did not follow Him?

The question is almost silly. Do my children always obey me? Well, they are good kids (probably better than most) but they aren't perfect. What do I do when they don't do what I've taught them? I disown them! I tell them I'm tired of their constant disobedience and I won't stand for it any more. I tell them to go out and find a new father.

Of course not! They are my daughters and there is absolutely nothing they can ever do to change that fact. I love them, and my love does not depend on their actions.

John Calvin, in the first volume of his *Institutes of the Christian Religion,* writes quite strongly about those who suggest that the only way to know you are a Christian is by your own righteousness. He puts it strongly but well:

> If you presume, says he [Peter Lombard], to hope for anything without merit, it should be called not hope, but presumption. Who, dear reader, does not execrate the gross stupidity which calls it rashness and presumption to con-

fide in the truth of God? The Lord desires us to expect everything from his goodness and yet these men tell us it is presumption to rest in it. O teacher, worthy of the pupils whom you found in these insane raving schools! Seeing that, by the oracles of God, sinners are enjoined to entertain the hope of salvation, let us willingly presume so far on this truth as to cast away all confidence in our works, and trusting in his mercy, venture to hope.[9]

Translation: Those who say that assurance of salvation has anything to do with our goodness are a bunch of turkeys.

In the seventh chapter of Romans Paul makes an amazing confession. Hardly anyone I know would ever make this kind of confession before a modern-day congregation. "For the good that I will to do, I do not do; but the evil I will not to do, that I practice. . . . So, then, with the mind I myself serve the law of God, but with the flesh the law of sin" (Rom. 7:19, 25). Do you think Paul for a moment doubted that he belonged to Christ? Listen to his words: "Who is he who condemns? It is Christ who died, and furthermore is also risen, who is even at the right hand of God, who also makes intercession for us. . . . For I am persuaded that . . . [nothing] shall be able to separate us from the love of God which is in Christ Jesus our Lord" (Rom. 8:34; 38–39).

If assurance of salvation could only be acquired by perceiving your goodness and knowing that it comes from God, Paul would have been unsure of his salvation. As a matter of fact, Paul's assurance of his salvation was, as a friend of mine says, irritating. "Nobody," my friend says, "should be that sure of being saved." And yet Paul was that sure. Why? Because he looked to Christ instead of to his own goodness.

The Law Doesn't Reflect the Heart

Third, it is inappropriate to use the law as a measure of spirituality. (The law can and often does measure our progress. However, when it is used as an outward measurement to show others our spirituality, it becomes inappropriate.) Jesus said about the Pharisees and scribes, "Woe to you, scribes and Pharisees, hypocrites! For you are like whitewashed tombs which indeed appear beautiful outwardly, but inside are full of dead men's bones and all uncleanness" (Matt. 23:27).

Have you ever met someone who did everything right? When they talk about sin, it is almost as if they are speaking as an outsider of the human race. Well, let me tell you something. As a pastor for over twenty-five years I know some of those people, and many of them are as mean as snakes. Their hearts are so distorted you wouldn't believe it. They do it right on the outside, but inside they are filled with bitterness, criticism, and hatred. Doing everything right is certainly no measurement of one's heart.

The Law Is Not a Weapon

Fourth, it is inappropriate to use the law as a weapon against other members of the family of God. Paul wrote, "Therefore you are inexcusable, O man, whoever you are who judge, for in whatever you judge another you condemn yourself; for you who judge practice the same things" (Rom. 2:1).

Listen, if you look for some bad things in me, you'll find them! And you aren't going to have to make them up, either. I'm better than I used to be, but I have so far to go that you won't have to work very hard to find something to criticize.

Lest you are already loading your gun, let me tell you something else. You aren't that hot yourself. In all honesty what we have here is a "Mexican Stand Off." We both have loaded guns, and we both make very good targets.

I often kid the congregation I serve by telling them, "Just before I retire I'm going to write a book, and the Sunday before I retire I will announce that fact from the pulpit with these words: 'My new book is going to be my experiences in the ministry. The book will contain names . . . and many of them are yours. But for a small contribution to my retirement fund, I will make sure your name is not in my new book.'" I always suggest that if I should do that, I would probably have a very comfortable retirement.

One elder caused me to stop using that "tongue in cheek" illustration. He said, "Pastor, I have known you for over fifteen years . . . and I might write a book too!"

The Law Does Not Make You Superior

Fifth, it is inappropriate to use the law as a way of setting ourselves on a pedestal with a divine calling to create others in our own image. It happens all the time. We have this cultural idea of what godly righteousness is, and we work to conform ourselves to it. Once we feel sufficiently superior to everyone else we go about making them like us.

That's what Paul was talking about when he wrote to the Galatians. Some very "spiritual" people had come into the congregation with a very specific agenda: to get the Galatians to turn from their freedom to a new conformity to the law. Paul writes: "O foolish Galatians! Who has bewitched you that you should not obey the truth, before whose eyes Jesus Christ was clearly portrayed among you as crucified? This only I want to learn from you: Did you receive the Spirit by the works of the law, or by the hearing of faith? Are you so foolish? Having begun in the Spirit, are you now being made perfect by the flesh?" (Gal. 3:1–3).

I think it would be a great gift to the church if God were to make us all wear neon signs listing our ten greatest sins for all the world to see.

You say, "You've got to be kidding! Everyone would know. It would be horrible for people to look at me and see all my sins!"

No, as a matter of fact, they wouldn't even be looking at your neon sign. They would be too busy trying to hide theirs. And then we would finally get honest. That wouldn't be half bad.

CHAPTER 8

WE
MUST
NEVER...
(Where to Draw the Line)

*"For you, brethren, have been called
to liberty; only do not use liberty as
an opportunity for the flesh."*
Galatians 5:13

I know what you said when you read the title of this chapter. If you're just getting into this thing about freedom in Christ, you're saying, "I knew it! I knew it! Here comes the catch. I thought this book was going to be different. Steve is just like the rest. You're free—but here are a few rules."

On the other hand, if you aren't into this freedom in Christ thing, you're saying, "I have been disturbed in spirit as I have read this book. Finally, in this chapter Steve is going to redeem his antinomian, heretical tendencies."

Wrong. Wrong. Wrong. You're both wrong!

I'm going to give you some biblical rules, but not the ones you think. Paul, in his great teaching on freedom and grace to the Galatians, says we are to be free, but we aren't to use our freedom as an opportunity for the flesh. The questions we must pose are: How can we use freedom as an opportunity for the flesh? What are the real dangers of the clear biblical teaching on freedom? Is there *any* place where we should draw the line? What is the difference between what Steve has written in this book and easy believism? If I really believe in the freedom Christ gives, how do I avoid antinomianism?

THE PRINCIPLES OF THE TRUTH

The best way to deal with those questions and others like them is to understand, when dealing with biblical freedom, that certain principles are always true. I call them rules, but you aren't going to be banned from the human race if you break them. They simply indicate the difference between biblical Christianity and something else. When you break the rules, you know something is going on which isn't of God. In other words, if you want to be a biblical Christian, there are certain signs of that reality. If those signs aren't present, then not only will you be an unhappy camper, but you may be in the wrong camp altogether. It may be a Christian camp, but it won't be a biblical one.

A pastor friend I'll call Bill loves to work with college students. One evening Bill came straight from campus to an evening meeting of the elders in his church. My friend has a rather bent sense of humor, and this evening was no exception.

"You guys would not believe what I just heard," my friend said as he took off his coat. "It was crazy! But we have a meeting to get to and you guys wouldn't be interested."

Everyone knows the best way to get someone's attention is to tell them a little bit of what could be a juicy story, and then tell them they wouldn't want to hear the rest. "Oh, we have time," one of the elders protested. "Tell us!"

"Well," Bill said reluctantly, "if you insist. This afternoon, some of the Christian kids were talking about Jesus. Do you know what they were saying?"

"No, what?"

"They were saying—I can hardly believe it—that Jesus is God. Can you believe they could be so naive? You'd think they had never read the Bible!"

Looking around the room, my friend continued, "What do you think about that?"

One elder began rather haltingly, "Well, that does sound crazy. But, on the other hand, you can't blame young people. It's the time in their lives when they can be wrong and it won't cost them anything."

"I can't believe they would think that!" another elder proclaimed.

"Bill," still another elder said, hesitantly, "I'm only a layman, and I don't know much about the Bible and all, but I sort of thought that Jesus was God."

As the discussion went around the room it became apparent that most of the elders were as disturbed as my friend about the college students' theology.

And then to everyone's surprise my friend got up from his chair, walked over to the coat rack, and started putting on his coat.

"Where are you going?" one of the elders asked.

"I'm getting out of here!" Bill exclaimed, starting for the door. "This is a meeting of the ruling board of this church, and you guys don't even know the central doctrine of the Christian faith. I've put my children under your direction, and I'm not even sure you're Christians."

Of course Bill, who is a Bible teacher, was making a very cogent point regarding the theological sophistication of those elders. Through that one incident he was able to teach in a way he never would have been able to teach in a sermon. When he finally took off his coat and sat back down, they were ready to listen.

We have this idea, at least in America, that it doesn't

really matter what you believe as long as you believe something and are sincere about it. I don't know about you, but I don't want to go to a nice, kind, sincere surgeon who believes he is right—but is wrong. He might amputate the wrong leg or take out my gall bladder when he was supposed to take out my appendix!

The Christian faith has to do with truth, but there is so much stuff around today that claims to be Christian and isn't, that believers must be very careful. For instance, there is a narrow, legalistic emphasis on holiness that is not Christianity—it's pharisaism. Sometimes the idea that God always wants His people to be happy is called Christian. It isn't. Some would label prosperity as the gospel, but it is often nothing but greed. With the advent of the New Age movement, some say that anything using the words "God" and "Jesus" must be Christian. As a matter of fact, some very shallow people have turned "God" and "Jesus' into mere concepts for their shallow religions.

The point is this: One of the dangers of this kind of teaching is that none of it is true apart from certain presuppositions which are also true. It's time to talk about those presuppositions, so, let's dig in.

Who Is a Christian?

First, we must never blur what ought to be a very clear line between the saved and the lost, the once born and the twice born, the slaves and the free. If you are not a Christian, you need to know that this book's message of freedom simply does not apply to you. You are still bound by a horrible kind of slavery to rules, regulations, and culture. Anybody who tells you any different has lied to you.

Paul, in his great work on freedom to the Galatians, was very worried about this issue. "But even if we, or an angel from heaven, preach any other gospel to you than what we have preached to you, let him be accursed. As we have said before, so now I say again, if anyone preaches any other gospel to you than what you have received, let him be accursed" (Gal. 1:8–9). Why do you think Paul repeated himself? Let me tell you. He wanted to be very clear on the gospel (good news) of Jesus Christ.

John, the apostle, writes, "They went out from us, but they were not of us" (1 John 2:19). In other words, there are those who use Christian words, go to Christian churches, say Christian prayers, and sing Christian hymns who are not Christians.

A lot of folks don't have any manifestation of the life of Christ in them simply because Christ isn't in them. They're pagans masking themselves as Christians. That's why it is desperately important that we make clear who is and who isn't a Christian. A Christian understands and accepts in a personal, existential way that Christ Jesus died for his or her sins and rests on that fact as the only hope of salvation.

One time the late Dr. Nelson Bell (Billy Graham's father-in-law and a great missionary statesman) was asked to speak before a rather liberal religious organization. The president of the organization, wary of Dr. Bell's evangelical stance, charged him, "Dr. Bell, I will expect you not to preach any of this 'born again' stuff. It is simply inappropriate here."

Dr. Bell respected the president's wishes and in his speech said nothing about being saved. However, the president had not mentioned the prayer—a serious oversight on his part. Dr. Bell prayed in closing, "Dear Lord, there are two kinds of people in this room—the saved and the lost. I pray that those who are lost will soon find Jesus Christ and accept Him as their Savior and the only way whereby they can be forgiven for their sins. I thank you that Christ died on a cross for our sins, and I ask that those who are lost would receive Him so that they might live forever. Amen."

We need to heed Dr. Bell's prayer. Without a clear demarcation between those who are Christians and those who aren't Christians, we will make false judgments regarding others' behavior. If a Christian seems to be making a mockery of his or her freedom in Christ, it may be a simple case of mistaken identity. In other words, that person may not be a Christian at all.

Our daughters had no rules when they were seniors in high school. Every year we very carefully removed a number of rules until there weren't any. Anna and I felt that it would be dangerous to have them move from total oversight (when they lived in our home) to total freedom (when they went off to college) without a transition period. We decided we'd rather let them try freedom at home so we could watch and help than to have them begin their lives of freedom away from us. By their last year of high school Robin and Jennifer had no curfew, no bed time, no dress code, no commandments about going to church or rules about music to which they could listen. They were really free.

You say, "Steve, that's crazy. I wouldn't do that with my daughter or son!"

I wouldn't do it with your daughter or son either. But these are our daughters and that made all the difference. Sometimes we bring kids into our home to live for a period of time when they are going through difficulties. I want you to know that they are given hardly any freedom. I watch them very carefully and make the rules very clear.

The difference between my children and someone else's

children is that my children are my children. Anna and I have loved them deeply, and they know it. We have instilled in them our spirit, and they know it. In removing the rules we knew that their relationship and fellowship with us was firmly established.

In the same way, if I am a true Christian, I am very much aware of God's love and what that love accomplished on the cross. Thus I am free to live in fellowship with God without any regulations. And that brings me to the second "we-must-never."

Limitless Love: The Motivating Force

Second, we must never limit the love of God. When Paul said that he was constrained by the love of Christ, he was talking about a reality that every Christian knows. Love, not fear, is the motivating force behind obedience. If we ever substitute fear for love, we have moved into something that isn't Christian. Not only that, if we substitute guilt, obligation, or appearances for love as motivating forces behind the Christian life, we will not only cease to live in a Christian way, but we will find people eventually turning away from even trying to live the Christian life. The process starts with the substitute and ends with desertion.

If I tell Robin and Jennifer, "I love you both, and as long as you live reasonably close to what I want for your life, I will continue to love you," or if I say, "There are some things that will cause me to stop loving you," how do you think they will react? They will live in fear and eventually become discouraged.

But if I say to them, "You are my daughters and there is nothing in the world that will ever cause me to stop loving you or which will cause you to no longer be my daughters—nothing," they are going to feel moved and constrained by my love.

Anna and I have told them, "There will be times when you do bad things. At those moments we want you to come to us, because only then will you really know that we love you. If you always did what we told you, you would think we loved you because you obeyed us. So always come to us, no matter what you have done, and you will know how much we love you."

We didn't come up with that idea by ourselves. We learned it from our heavenly Father who said the same thing to us in Christ: "My love is without limit. You can never do anything to make me stop loving you." If we ever soften that, we will have ceased being Christian, and those who come to us would be just as happy with Islam or Buddhism.

The Importance of Holiness

Third, we must never soften the clear teaching of the law of God. The Christian faith is not a methodology to help wild, disobedient swingers do whatever they want and still feel good about themselves. When Paul said that we must never use our liberty as an opportunity for the flesh, he was saying, in effect, that those who do, haven't understood.

I get criticized for particular sermons I preach. (Anybody who says they like criticism will lie about other things too.) Some people criticize my sermons because they don't like me or anything for which I stand. When those people come to me with their spurious "godly correction," I usually tell them to go hang it on their ear and that it will get very cold in a very hot place before I change my sermon to accommodate their narrow, unsophisticated, unbiblical views.

But other folks love me. I have experienced their love and concern, and they have earned the right to be heard. I can't say that I like criticism or that when they criticize me I thank them and change immediately. But I'll tell you this, when people who love me criticize me, I listen. I have a friend who has earned, with his love, the right to say anything to me. Recently he told me I should take a certain sermon and "put it on the bottom of the pile." Guess what? I put it on the bottom of the pile!

When I became a Christian two things happened. I got saved and I got loved. I got loved so deeply that it still amazes me when I think about it. Because I got loved so deeply, I want to please the One who loved me that much. I may not always please Him—sometimes I even run in the other direction, because His love can really hurt. I may chafe against pleasing Him; I may find myself in a very far country; I may not even speak to Him. But I'll tell you something: I want to please Him and when I don't please Him it hurts.

Now if I really want to please Him, I must know what pleases Him. I find that out by reading the Word and listening to His commandments. When I know what He wants, I want what He wants. Love does that to you. But I must know what He wants. That is why we must never soften the teaching of the law of God. Holiness is a very important teaching as long as it is given in the context of God's love.

The Reality of Disobedience

Fourth, we must never pretend that the world is any different than it really is. If you read the chapter in this book on the law of God, you know that the law is given to show us the best way to live. God doesn't sit around trying to dream up the best ways to make us miserable. The law reflects the way the world works in the same way an instruction manual for a computer explains how the computer programs work. You can ignore the instructions, but the programs won't run.

If God, who loves us, has given us an instruction manual, and we ignore the instructions, we have no right to complain because we are miserable and hurt. I don't know about you, but I'm tired of Christians who sow their wild oats and pray for a crop failure.

It should not surprise anyone that Paul, toward the end of his magnificent teaching on freedom, should say, "Do not be deceived, God is not mocked; for whatever a man sows, that he will also reap" (Gal. 6:7). We need to be just as clear on that as Paul was. If you jump off a ten-story building, there is going to be an abrupt, painful stop. That's just how things are. If you disobey God's laws with impunity, you're going to get hurt. That's just how things are.

When everything is messed up because people wanted to do it their way rather than God's way, we need to be able to say, "Look. Don't whine. We told you that God has given instructions. If you don't obey them, don't be surprised if the thing doesn't work."

But we need also, when someone hasn't obeyed the instructions, to let them know that they have a grand opportunity to experience Christ's love and grace. If we don't tell them that, we will be giving only half of the message. And that brings me to another "we-must-never."

The Presence of the Holy Spirit

Fifth, we must never forget about the Holy Spirit. In John 16 Jesus is telling His disciples that He is going away. They are not very happy about the prospect, so Jesus tells them: "Nevertheless I tell you the truth. It is to your advantage that I go away; for if I do not go away, the Helper will not come to you; but if I depart, I will send Him to you. And when He has come, He will convict the world of sin, and of righteousness, and of judgment: of sin, because they do not believe in Me; of righteousness, because I go to My Father and you see Me no more; of judgment, because the ruler of this world is judged. I still have many things to say to you, but you cannot bear them now. However, when He, the Spirit of truth, has come, He will guide you into all truth; for He will not speak on His own authority, but whatever He hears He will speak; and He will tell you things to come. He will glorify Me, for He will take of what is Mine and declare it to you" (John 16:7–14).

How about that, sports fans?

I thought all that was *my* job. I'll bet, if you are a mature Christian, you thought it was your job too. Almost everything we do wrong in regard to freedom—judging other people, trying to get them to fit our Christian mold, telling them what they ought and ought not do, deciding on whether they are good enough to be called a part of our family, being overly concerned with our witness in the community—is the business of the Holy Spirit.

I remember the first time I had a secretary. I had been serving a small church on Cape Cod where the pastor did it all: typed the letters, prepared the bulletin, worked the mimeograph, and answered the phone. (I almost said made the coffee, but that would be sexist, so I won't say it.) I wasn't too skilled at those things, but nobody else was around to do them, so I was elected.

When I became the pastor of a larger church, I continued trying to do all those things. Guess what happened? The church secretary had to train me. Her name was Mrs. Kelsey, and she came to me one day and said, "Mr. Brown, I'm getting rather uncomfortable."

I told her to sit down and we would talk about it.

She was hardly seated before she started talking. "I have a job description here, and you keep fulfilling my job description. My concern is the church, and if we can save some money, I will be glad to look for another job. However, to be perfectly honest with you, you are not doing my job very well. In fact, you are making a mess of it. So, either fire me or use me."

She then taught me how to dictate and delegate and trust her to do her job. It was wonderful!

But it wasn't half as wonderful as the discovery that I was doing the Holy Spirit's job and didn't have to. Our Lord the Holy Spirit is perfectly capable of leading Christians in the right direction. He is also perfectly capable of convicting them and of motivating them to do what the Father wants them to do.

I don't know about you, but for me that is a great relief. Someone once told a man who had said he was "self-made" that he relieved God of a tremendous responsibility! Well, I don't want to be self-made. I don't want the people I teach and pastor to be self-made or Steve-made. I want them to be filled with the Holy Spirit.

The Freedom in Grace

Finally, we must never soften the clear teaching of the Bible on grace. Paul in his teaching on freedom speaks of those people who had come into the congregations at Galatia and caused a number of people (including his young friend Titus) to be confused about their liberty. Paul writes, "And this occurred because of false brethren secretly brought in (who came in by stealth to spy out our liberty which we have in Christ Jesus, that they might bring us into bondage), to whom we did not yield submission even for an hour, that the truth of the gospel might continue with you" (Gal. 2:4–5).

I can understand those who came into the churches at Galatia and tried to get the people away from Paul's teaching. If I had been a church leader, I probably would have at least thought about doing the same thing.

I hope I would not have done it dishonestly. I hope I would have gone to Paul and tried to reason with him. I would have said, "Paul, I too love the fact of my freedom, but these folks are going to leave the faith altogether. They are just not mature enough for your kind of teaching. We need to establish some rules and tell them that God's holiness will eat them alive if they get out of line. After all, Paul, we need to maintain the proper Christian witness in the community. We must remember that when Christ calls us He bids us come and die. Paul, don't bring shame on Christ by allowing too much freedom. Those folks are not as mature as you are. They will just use their freedom as an excuse to swing."

That seems to me like a perfectly reasonable and logical way to deal with the problem. Only the Bible and experience tell me that it just doesn't work. In fact, it has just the opposite effect from what Christian leaders desire for their followers.

I've given you the principle earlier, and we must never forget it: obedience comes through freedom, not freedom through obedience. We must never soften the teach-

ing of grace, lest we miss the joy God has promised.
Dale Padgett, a friend of mine, expresses the joy:

Freedom
blossoms in my soul and spirit,
opening petal by petal from the bud of God's Word.
Freedom
leads me by the hand,
holding tightly to my own steady, firm grip.
Freedom
calls me by name,
beckoning away from expectations and complications.
Freedom
pulls on my heartstrings,
guiding toward a simplified, truthful spirituality.
Freedom
dances through my bones,
laughing with my own eagerness to respond.
Freedom
paints itself across my mind,
filling the canvas with smiling peace.
Freedom
sings in the silence,
echoing a melody of deeply breathed joy.
Freedom
enters in the name of Jesus,
speaking, singing, shouting, celebrating
its way into the hearts and souls of seekers.

That's it! "Well," you say, "if that's what it is, why don't
I experience it?" Funny you should ask. In the third sec-
tion of the book the question before the house will be: If
I'm so free, why do I feel so bound?

Part Three

IF JESUS HAS SET ME FREE, WHY DO I FEEL SO BOUND?

CHAPTER 9

STRANGER THAN FICTION
(Christians Who Like to Be Bound)

"And Moses said to Pharaoh, 'Accept the honor of saying when I shall intercede for you, for your servants, and for your people, to destroy the frogs from you and your houses, that they may remain in the river only.' So he said, 'Tomorrow.'"

Exodus 8:9–10a

People are funny. Consider the eighth chapter of Exodus, where Moses is trying to get Pharaoh to allow the people of God to leave Egypt. Pharaoh has a labor problem and, as management, is not about to cave in to labor's demands. But Moses has some rather extraordinary help in the wings, so the issue has already been decided—Pharaoh just doesn't know it yet.

You will remember that God inflicted a number of plagues on the Egyptians, each geared to bring Pharaoh to an affirmative decision to release the people of God. The incident ends, as they always do, with God getting His way.

One of the plagues was a plague of frogs. Now this wasn't just a couple of frogs. We're talking about a whole lot of frogs. "So the river shall bring forth frogs abundantly, which shall go up and come into your house, into your bedroom, on your bed, into the houses of your servants, on your people, into your ovens, and into your kneading bowls" (Ex. 8:3).

Not even a frog collector wants that many frogs. Can you imagine getting into your bed and finding frogs under the sheets? How long can you eat frog bread? Everywhere you stepped, you would hear the squish of mashed frogs. Yuck!

It should be no surprise to anyone that Pharaoh summoned Moses and Aaron and asked them to call off the frogs. What is really a surprise is that when Moses asked

Pharaoh when he wanted the frogs out, Pharaoh answered, "Tomorrow."

Tomorrow? Pharaoh, are you crazy? Have you got a frog fixation? Have you gotten used to the squish? What do you mean, tomorrow?

I'll never understand Pharaoh, but as a pastor I have learned to accept a lot of strange behavior. I suppose I could accept Pharaoh's too, but I sure would like to ask him about it. I suspect his answers would be about as bizarre as his behavior.

If you have managed to make your way this far into this book, you must have some questions. Let me guess. The first question surely is this: If the law reflects the parameters of God's desire, not His love, why are Christians still bound? Why do Christians live as if keeping the rules will help them gain God's love? The answer: People are funny. Let me explain.

WHY STAY IN THE PRISON?

In an interview, F. F. Bruce, a retired professor from Manchester University in England and the author of some forty books and nearly two thousand articles and reviews, was asked: "We have noticed that though many Christians adhere to Paul, they do not live lives characterized by Paul's theology of freedom. How do you resolve this apparent contradiction?"

Dr. Bruce answered,

> If they are obviously not free, they don't adhere to Paul! They may think they do, but they haven't begun to learn what Paul means by 'the liberty with which Christ has set His people free' (Gal. 5:1).
>
> Many people, including many Christians, are afraid of liberty. They are afraid of having too much liberty them-

selves; and they're certainly afraid of letting other people, especially younger people, have too much liberty. Think of the dangers that liberty might lead them into! It seems much better to move in predestinate grooves.[10]

While I appreciate Dr. Bruce's comments and agree with them, he didn't answer the question. He just restated the problem. I understand his dilemma. If you deal with people very much you sometimes just have to accept the fact that people are funny and you'll never fully understand them.

But the question still haunts the back burner of my mind. Why wouldn't people want to be free? One would think, given the fact that I am not saying anything new in this book and that God is quite clear about freedom and grace in the Bible, that every Christian in the world would at least get this one point right. After all, this is what the Christian faith is all about. The gospel is called good news because it is.

Remember the man Jesus healed at the Sheep Gate Pool? The man had been a cripple for thirty-eight years and had come to the pool to be healed. John wrote, "When Jesus saw him lying there, and knew that he already had been in that condition a long time, He said to him, 'Do you want to be made well?'" (John 5:6).

There was a time when I would have thought Jesus' question was dumb at best. But as a matter of fact, most people decide to stay the way they are. There are reasons, sometimes even unconscious ones, people make debilitating decisions about their lives.

That is no less true in the area of Christian freedom. People are living in a prison and have been given the key to their cell door, yet they hide the key and pretend that nothing can be done. The question: Why?

I suspect there are many reasons why people don't unlock the door, and this chapter by no means will exhaust the list. However, as an observer in the prison, I have discovered some things about prisoners that might help. (I've spent quite some time in the Christian "slammer" myself.) Let's go down some roads that both you and I may have traveled to the prison. If we can find where we got off track, maybe we can find our way back.

The Security of the Cell

First, there is a certain amount of security in being a prisoner. Remember what God's people said to Moses as they stood on the shores of the Red Sea? They didn't bother to thank him for leading them out of slavery. Instead, they muttered and complained: "Because there were no graves in Egypt, have you taken us away to die in the wilderness? Why have you so dealt with us, to bring us up out of Egypt? Is this not the word that we told you in Egypt, saying, 'Let us alone that we may serve the Egyptians?' For it would have been better for us to serve the Egyptians than that we should die in the wilderness" (Ex. 14:11–12).

All of us like to be secure. That's why, given the choice between anarchy and totalitarianism, human beings will choose totalitarianism every time. The freedom we, in North America, enjoy is in great danger. As our society moves more and more away from its necessary component of individual responsibility, we will call for a dictator who can deal with the problems of crime, violence, pollution, and dishonesty. It isn't that we like dictators. It's just that in our humanness we will choose security even above freedom itself if we can't have both. We will cry out, as did the elders of Israel, "Now make us a king to judge us like all the [other] nations" (1 Sam. 8:5).

If I'm in prison, the walls keep out the bad things I fear. My life is programmed by others and my needs are met. I often speak in prisons and I have found an interesting phenomenon there—prisoners who like being in prison. In fact, it is not uncommon for prisoners, once released, to commit a crime in order to return to prison. Making a living, fighting for a place, struggling to deal with the complications and contradictions of freedom is not altogether pleasant for anyone.

Fred Smith, author of *You and Your Network* and a columnist for *Leadership* magazine, tells of the time his daughter said to him, "My friends have everything. They get whatever they want whenever they want it."

Fred, thinking that the whole speech was a ploy to get something, asked, "And what does that say about them?"

His daughter replied, "It says that their parents don't love them."

Every child needs security. A lot of adolescent rebellion is actually a cry for the security of parameters. Discipline is the way parents can provide the security of love—and, believe it or not, kids know it.

The problem is that our need for security sometimes robs us of our heritage of freedom. Wouldn't you like to live in a place where you were always safe from outsiders and where you had plenty to eat and a job from which you would never be fired? Wouldn't it be nice to always have adequate medical care, free clothing, and entertainment? We would all like that security sometimes. But forever?

That's called a prison.

Our counterfeit Christian faith can become a prison. We can let someone else think for us, know and live by the rules, and be secure—looking, thinking, and acting like the other prisoners. There is a lot of comfort in that, and to be perfectly honest with you, I look back to that prison at times with a nostalgia in my heart. But my head (and the Bible) tells me that is totally inappropriate.

Getting What We Deserve

Second, a lot of us won't use Jesus' key to get out of the prison because we think we deserve to stay there. I would suggest that we have drawn a false conclusion from a fact. The fact is "all have sinned and fallen short of the glory of God" (Rom. 3:23). The false conclusion is "all will be punished." We assume sin and punishment go together— "all have sinned so all will be punished"—and send ourselves to the prison of punishment. We forget that Christ, in His role as priest, received the punishment for sin and set the prisoners free.

I hate to have someone pay my way. I'm a better giver than receiver. I recognize that receiving is as much an art as giving, but it is still hard for me. Every once in a while I will go to a restaurant in our city where a waiter or waitress or manager knows me. When I go to pay my check, the cashier says, "Your bill has already been paid."

That really gets under my skin. (I know, I know. My attitude is something less than gracious. God isn't through with me yet.) I simply can't stand *not* to pay. My Protestant work ethic says if you owe it, you pay it.

I'm the same way about paying for my sin. I'm guilty. I know I'm a sinner. The Bible told me, and besides, I knew it even before I read the Bible. That means that I need to balance the books, and doggone it, I'm going to stay in prison until every book is balanced and every debt paid. Never mind that Jesus has already balanced the books and paid the debt. Never mind that I have the key in my pocket. Never mind that Jesus has asked me to come out of prison. I owe, I owe, I owe . . . and off to jail I go.

Let me show you the healthy process of acknowledging sin that enables us to work through our feelings of guilt. There are four steps: violation, shame (or guilt), punishment, and freedom.

You can best see the system at work in children because they haven't had time to learn adult strategies such as dishonesty and rationalization, to cover their tracks. A boy disobeys his mother (violation), and he really feels bad about it (shame and guilt). So finally, after time passes, he is either caught or he tells his mother he has disobeyed her. She reprimands him or spanks him (punishment), and then he feels good again (freedom). That system is quite healthy.

In our society the word *punishment* has developed some unfortunate negative connotations. It is a good word and it implies a good result. Punishment balances societies' books, and it balances our personal psychological books when the punishment is commensurate with the crime or sin.

As members of a community or a family, we need to be punished for wrongdoing. One of the most dangerous movements in our society is the development of prisons as mere places for rehabilitation. As a matter of fact, we do great harm to criminals when we don't grant them the opportunity to, as it were, balance the books. Rehabilitation is not wrong, but the best rehabilitation takes place when we understand the prison system as retributive *and* rehabilitative. (In fact, if we were more biblical we would have fewer people in prison. They would be out paying back their victims.) If we understood the necessity of retributive justice, prisoners would be moving toward emotional as well as physical freedom. After serving their time, they would have made restitution, and they would truly be free. Punishment has received a bad rap in our society. But those who understand human nature (others' and their own) know there is a lot to be said on behalf of punishment.

In fact, punishment does balance the books and, once the books have been balanced, we are free. Parents who don't understand that will cause themselves a lot of trouble. A society that doesn't understand it will cause everybody else a lot of trouble.

But what if you have done things that can't be repaired? What if, even after you spent a thousand years working, you could never repay the debt?

That's our predicament according to the Bible: We owe more than we can ever repay. Once we move from a violation of parental or societal law (those areas where there is a possibility of repayment), there is a whole different set of circumstances.

A priest dreamed he was called before the judgment seat of God. He expected a big book and a big God reading from it. Instead, in his dream, he saw a gigantic pair of scales. On one side the angels were piling up the good he had done, and on the other side the demons were piling up the bad he had done. He had done a lot of good. After all, he was a priest. But, to his horror, he noticed that the angels simply couldn't keep up. They didn't have the material. The scales began to tip quickly to the bad side. He cried out, "Oh, Christ, have mercy!"

At that moment, he heard the sound of three blood-stained nails falling on the good side. They didn't look that heavy. After all, how much could three nails weigh? But as they dropped onto the scales, the scales tipped back to the good side and no matter what the demons added, they stayed there. Those nails, of course, were the nails driven through the hands and feet of Jesus Christ.

You don't deserve to be free? Of course, you don't. You don't deserve to be loved? Of course, you don't. Your bad self-image is the result of your sin? Of course, it is. You feel that whatever punishment you receive, you had it coming? Of course, you did. With Oswald Chambers you cry out, "Now I must dwell in tears."

No, you don't! You are free because Christ on the cross made you free. You are valuable because He says you are valuable. You don't "have anything coming" because He took it all. You don't have to dwell forever in tears, because, to paraphrase Scripture, He who was joyful became sad that by His sadness you might have joy (2 Cor. 8:9).

But there are other reasons some people choose the prison. For instance, some choose the chains because their self-image is so horrible that they don't expect anything else. They say to themselves, "My background is miserable, my friends think I'm miserable, my spouse thinks I'm miserable, my marriage is miserable, my work is miserable. There is no reason my Christian faith shouldn't make me miserable too. That's the way things are." As someone has said, "I've been down so long that even up looks like it's down."

We had a German shepherd once (his name was Calvin and he is in doggy heaven) who had been horribly beaten by a previous owner. He just showed up on our doorstep and the women in my family took him in because they take in anything that is hurt. So Calvin became our protector. The problem was, so the vet said, that Calvin couldn't even protect himself. When trouble came, he just crawled over in the corner and whined.

Every time I tried to pet Calvin, he thought I was going to hit him. He would run or cower on the floor, waiting for my blow. I tried to tell him I would never hit him. I tried to explain to him that I loved him and that he was now a part of the Brown family and that Browns didn't hit up on Browns. I tried to convince him that I was different than his previous owner. But Calvin would have none of it. I was a cruel, angry, mean master, and nothing would change his mind.

One of the things the vet told me about Calvin was that you could tell a lot about a dog owner by examining the dog. (That's how he knew Calvin had been beaten by the previous owner.) If you judged Jesus by some of His followers, you would think Jesus must be some kind of horrible person.

Listen to what the Bible says:

> I sought the Lord, and He heard me,
> And delivered me from all my fears.
> They looked to Him and were radiant,
> And their faces were not ashamed.
> This poor man cried out, and the Lord heard him,
> And saved him out of all his troubles.
> The angel of the Lord encamps all around those
>   who fear Him,
> And delivers them.
> Oh, taste and see that the Lord is good;
> Blessed is the man who trusts in Him! (Ps. 34:4–8)

If you are a believer and you haven't seen the reality of a benevolent God, you haven't changed owners. Once you belonged to Satan. Don't let the patterns you developed under him continue under the new owner. The New Owner loves you. Just taste and see.

I don't know about you, but I'm tired of people who make the major work of redemption a good Christian self-image. However, a good self-image is a by-product of the work of Christ. Why? Because your value has been determined, not by the world or the church or your Christian friends, but by the God of the universe who sent His Son to a cross because you were that important. A good self-image reflects how valuable you believe you are. When you understand the great value God has placed on you, it does wonders for your self-image. If the fact that God has made you valuable doesn't help your attitude and your self-image, then go ahead and stay in the prison. Just quit complaining about it.

Playing It Safe

There is a fourth reason why Christians refuse to use the key Jesus has given them. They are afraid to risk. Paul said, "For God has not given us a spirit of fear" (2 Tim. 1:7). That sounds good, but many Christians simply have never claimed the promise for themselves and are not sure, if they are honest, that it is true.

We have seen that a lot of people are not free because they have a great need for security. They are afraid to take risks.

Religion (any religion) has a positive influence on culture in that it preserves traditional, shared, societal values. That's good. The Christian faith is no exception. One of the major problems we are facing in Western civilization is the great loss of a shared system of values.

That, of course, is another subject altogether. But for the purposes of this book, we need to see that the down side, the conservative nature of religion and religious people, is to play it safe. Within certain parameters, that's a very good trait. But it tends to produce neurotic Christians if we aren't careful.

Christians should serve their country by affirming traditional and biblical values. That is our gift to our country. But when that gift becomes an excuse for conformity, we haven't understood what Christ meant by freedom. When the gift we offer our nation becomes another way to play it safe we will be offering, not a gift, but a prison.

I have a friend whose mother lived in constant fear that something bad was going to happen to him. He was not allowed out of her sight. He couldn't ride a bicycle or play ball because he might get hurt. He couldn't have very many friends because they were a bad influence. When he went to school, it had to be a private school because the public schools would destroy him. When all his friends got their driver's licenses, his mother told him he was too young and driving was too dangerous.

I suspect some really bad psychological themes were playing in his mother's head, but she was not so different from what mother church has done to a lot of her children. As a result, we have created a militarily defensible system whereby we can protect ourselves against the dangers of the outside world.

Risk is simply not in the vocabulary of most cultural Christianity. What do you think would happen if you said what you thought for a change? What if you befriended a few pagans? What if you asked a question or expressed doubt? Do you think God might strike you down if you read something other than a Christian book? What if you didn't go to that meeting—just once? What if you didn't obey all the rules (I'm not talking about the ones in the Bible) for once?

"I know what would happen," you say. "Everyone is depending on me. But more important than that, God is depending on me."

"What you mean to say," I would respond, "is that you are afraid of what would happen."

"I don't know if I would describe it as 'fear,' but, now that you mention it. . . ."

So, what do you do? You risk! You'll never know how exciting it is to be free until, despite your fear, you step out in that freedom. You'll make a wonderful discovery: there really is a God and everything didn't fall apart. God will be there providing the safety net. You will find that all the horrible things you expected to happen didn't. And then you'll ask yourself, "Why didn't I do it before?"

Keeping Control

A fifth reason we don't use the key Jesus gave us is that we want to be in control. Now being in a prison doesn't sound like you are in control until you think about it a bit. When you're in prison your environment is small. So are the demands. I can control a prison cell.

I was once offered the pulpit of a rather large church. I called my friend Dr. Aiken Taylor (whose passing has added an attraction to heaven) and asked him about this particular church. He exclaimed, "You're crazy! That church is so big it will be like getting on a train. You don't change the direction of a train; you get on, you get off, or you get run over. You would be miserable."

Dr. Taylor was right. As long as it is small, I have some measure of control. If it gets big, I might lose control. Prison cells are not very pleasant places, but they are small. And if we stay in the cell, we can at least keep our hand on everything in that cell.

I would like to preach against alcoholic beverages. Drunkenness is a horrible sin, and I can wax eloquent on its horrors. I'm a teetotaler, and I can give forth wonderful and spiritual reasons why Christians ought to practice total abstinence. But if I am honest, the real reason I don't drink alcoholic beverages is that if I did, I could get drunk, and if I got drunk, I might lose control. Don't get me wrong; I'm glad I don't drink, but the truth is that I hate the thought of losing control.

But here's the point: control is an illusion—even in a prison cell. The psalmist realized this when he asked God,

> Where can I go from Your Spirit?
> Or where can I flee from Your presence?
> If I ascend into heaven, You are there;
> If I make my bed in hell, behold, You are there.
> If I take the wings of the morning,
> And dwell in the uttermost parts of the sea,
> Even there Your hand shall lead me,
> And Your right hand shall hold me. (Ps. 139:7–10)

Do you see it? God is in control in the prison cell and in the castle. He controls your coming in and your going out, wherever you are. Why not go out into the sunshine and let Him worry about controlling things? He does a rather good job of it.

In *The Last Battle,* by C. S. Lewis, Aslan the Lion, who represents Christ, is asked by Lucy to help some dwarfs who, even inside the door of Narnia, which is heaven, think they are in a black hole. They simply refuse to believe that Aslan has come and that they are free to enjoy Narnia. They misinterpret any signs Aslan gives them. Instead, they just wander around in their supposed darkness. Aslan shows Lucy that he can do nothing to help them:

> "Dearest," said Aslan, "I will show you both what I can and cannot do." He came close to the Dwarfs and gave a long growl: low, but it set the air shaking. But the Dwarfs said to one another, "Hear that? That's the gang at the other end of the stable. Trying to frighten us. They do it

with a machine of some kind. Don't take any notice. They won't take us in again!"

Aslan raised his head and shook his mane. Instantly a glorious feast appeared on the Dwarfs' knees: pies and tongues and pigeons and trifles and ices, and each Dwarf had a goblet of good wine in his right hand. But it wasn't much use. They began eating and drinking greedily enough, but it was clear that they couldn't taste it properly. They thought they were eating and drinking only the sort of things you might find in a stable. One said he was trying to eat hay and another said he had got a piece of an old turnip and a third said he'd found a raw cabbage leaf. And they raised golden goblets of rich red wine to their lips and said, "Ugh! Fancy drinking dirty water out of a trough that a donkey's been at! Never thought we'd come to this." But very soon every Dwarf began suspecting that every other Dwarf had found something nicer than he had, and they started grabbing and snatching, and went on to quarrelling, till in a few minutes there was a free fight and all the good food was smeared on their faces and clothes or trodden under foot. But when at last they sat down to nurse their black eyes and their bleeding noses, they all said:

"Well, at any rate there's no Humbug here. We haven't let anyone take us in. The Dwarfs are for the Dwarfs."

"You see," said Aslan. "They will not let us help them. They have chosen cunning instead of belief. Their prison is only in their own minds, yet they are in that prison . . . But come, children. I have other work to do."[11]

Oh, yes, there is another reason Christians stay in the prison, even with the key in their pocket: They have made some horrible assumptions about the prison keepers and the prisoners. Turn the page and we'll talk about it.

CHAPTER 10

WHAT THE PRISON KEEPERS DON'T TELL YOU
(Secrets That Can Change Your Life)

*"I could wish that those who trouble you
would even cut themselves off! For you,
brethren, have been called to liberty."*
                                    Galatians 5:12–13

I spoke at a conference in a large church where a friend of mine is pastor. At the end of the week my friend decided to take me to the airport himself so we would have time to talk. I was curious. Didn't my friend have more important things to do than take speakers to the airport?

While we stopped for coffee, he began, "Steve, how do you get away with saying the things you say in the pulpit? As I listened to you I kept thinking, 'I don't believe he should have said that.' In fact, if I had said some of the things you said, I would be fired."

"And yet," he continued, looking down at his coffee cup, "I looked at my congregation, thinking they would be offended and angry. They weren't. They were right with you! I'm afraid to say the kinds of things you say because of what would happen if I said them."

"Sam" (not his name), I replied, "you don't like yourself very much, do you?"

"How do you know that?" he countered. Few would have suspected this, because he is one of the most winsome, articulate pastors I know. His church is very large, his wife is beautiful, and he is the envy of almost every other pastor who knows him.

His question deserved an answer, and I gave it to him. "Sam, I can tell you don't like yourself because you are very much afraid that people won't like you. If you don't like yourself, and people don't like you, then nobody likes you, and you couldn't stand that. You're afraid if you risk offending people, they wouldn't like you."

"Dear me," my friend hardly knows any words stronger than that and, if he did, he wouldn't use them because someone might not like him. "That hurt."

"And there's another reason I know what you're feeling."

"What's that?"

"It takes one to know one. The only difference between you and me is that I'm a little older and farther down the road than you are. I've started to risk and have discovered a great secret."

"What's that?"

"That God really is there and when I risk, He provides the safety net. I've also discovered that I'm not a half bad person, and that some people like me even when I don't do what they want me to do. And there's another thing."

"What's that?"

"I've discovered that the others don't matter. An English proverb I like has helped me a lot."

"What's that?" (My friend has a rather limited vocabulary.)

"Fear knocked at the door, and nobody was there."

We talked a lot about our fear, and we are now cheerleaders for each other. We're both discovering that the only way to be free is to risk, and the more we risk, the freer we become. Who knows? One of these days we might be able to walk away from the prison and never look back.

It would be nice to get away from the prison, wouldn't it? Maybe you can identify with Sam, even if you aren't a preacher. Maybe you, too, would like to be free but don't know how to go about it.

THE SECRETS ABOUT THE PRISONERS AND THE PRISON KEEPERS

In this chapter I'm going to share some secrets free people already know. If you haven't discovered how wonderful it is to be free, you'll just have to trust me. (Would a pastor lie to you? Never mind. Don't answer that.) Rather than just trust me, check it out for yourself and see if I'm right. You're in for a wonderful treat.

I'm going to tell you something about the prison keepers and the other prisoners that you wouldn't have believed if I hadn't told you and you hadn't checked. I still have trouble believing it myself.

Prison keepers are pretty scary people. In fact, if it weren't for them, we would probably be free. If we weren't afraid of what others thought and said about us, we would probably be quite free. It behooves us then, to make sure we understand those people who keep us from being free.

Let's talk about the secrets of the prison keepers and the prisoners.

You Are Not Alone

First of all, they are just like you. If you read Charles Spurgeon's book *Lectures to My Students*,[12] and if you know anything about preachers and seminary students, you'll think, "How contemporary and relevant he is for today's seminary students! He lived a hundred years ago, yet his material is just as relevant as it was the day he gave it."

Do you know why Spurgeon is as relevant today as he

was in the nineteenth century? Because he understood something many of us have forgotten: Human beings are human beings and truth is truth. Spurgeon understood that if he preached and spoke to his own heart and ministry, he would hit everyone else's heart and ministry too.

I have an advantage over most of you: I'm a pastor and therefore people open their hearts to me and tell me what they really think. Guess what I've discovered? They feel as guilty as I do. They, too, wake up scared in the middle of the night. They, too, become insecure and lonely in a crowd. And they, too, are afraid of what people will say about them.

A number of years ago a friend of mine told me if I wanted to overcome my nervousness in front of large crowds, I should picture the audience in their underwear. (I still get nervous, but I have this tendency to giggle a lot.) Do you know that everybody looks funny in their underwear? It sort of makes everybody even. They don't look quite so judgmental and angry in their underwear. Try to remember that. You'll be amazed at how much freer you are when you realize that everyone is just like you.

No One Is Perfect

The second secret is like the first: There are no super-prisoners or super-prison keepers in the prison. For years I thought that somewhere there must be people who didn't have any problems and who could tell me how to be perfect. I thought if I could only find them, I would do whatever they told me. I'm still looking.

Now that doesn't mean there aren't Christians who have gone further than I have or who are more mature than I am. It doesn't mean I can't have mentors and advisors. It does mean, however, that all the Christian leaders I have ever met bleed just as I bleed and have problems just as I have problems.

I've always wanted to be a great golfer. I have taken lessons, watched videos, read books, practiced, and (as a last resort) prayed. All those things (contrary to what my friends think) have helped. But do you know what has helped my golf game more than anything? On television I saw Arnie Palmer hit a ball into the woods. Not only that, he and his caddy had trouble finding it.

That was the day I got free on the golf course. If Arnie Palmer blows it sometimes, then I know it's okay if I blow it. It's amazing how comforting that thought really is.

The problem in the church is that we have never seen (either because many of them won't let us see or because we don't want to see) our leaders blow it. They're afraid to blow it because, if they do, their followers will fire them. We're afraid to see them blow it because it's important to us that our leaders always do it right.

I spent a lot of time talking about this problem in my book *No More Mr. Nice Guy!* so I'm not going to spend that much time on it here. (This, of course, is a rather questionable way to get you to buy another one of my books.) You might want to read the chapter in that book titled "God and the Gurus" for more detail. But let me say here that we often foster the lie that super-prisoners and super-prison keepers exist in order to feed our neurotic need to have someone over us telling us what to do—or to be over someone telling them what to do. We ignore their faults, glamorize their lives with unrealistic biographies, and worship their greatness. Pretty soon we have idols and the idols have power. We consider these to be good relationships because some people like to tell others what to do and some people are neurotic enough to like to be told what to do.

Jesus was rather hard on those who presumed to be super-prison keepers. "You know that the rulers of the Gentiles lord it over them, and those who are great exercise authority over them. Yet it shall not be so among you; but whoever desires to become great among you, let him be your servant. And whoever desires to be first among you, let him be your slave" (Matt. 20:25–27).

I know of nothing that has caused more trouble for the Christian church in America than our "super-Christian" mentality. Every time someone comes to me as if I were a "super-Christian," wanting me to direct their life, I say something very pastoral, like, "Do I look like your mother?" Once that is settled, we can sit down and together go before the Father. Once that is settled, I am willing to be a pastor—not a guru.

To those of you who have a Christian hero who tells you what to do and what not to do, let me give you a word of biblical advice: Don't let them do it to you. To those of you who are Christian leaders and have found that people force you into a role that belongs only to God and your mother, let me give you a word of biblical advice: Don't let them do it to you.

Everyone Wants to Be Free

Third, not only are the prison keepers and the other prisoners just like you, but they would be just as happy as you to get out of the prison.

Did you hear the story about the drummer in the mission band who was asked to give his testimony on a street corner at Christmas? Stepping in front of the band, he started boldly: "There was a time in my life when all I did was go to parties and run around and gamble and drink and look for excitement. . . ."

Just then the expression on his face changed and he paused. When he started again, it was not what anyone expected. He said, "And now all I do is beat this stupid drum."

Of course, I wouldn't suggest that we Christians go back to our old pagan life. But we know life ought to be a whole lot better than it is now. It is getting to the point where we need testimonies for three stages of Christian growth: first, how Christ saved us from the pagans; second, how He saved us from the Christians; and third, how Christ brought us to Himself.

Do you know those horrible people who judge you all the time? They want to be free just like you do. Do you know those Christian leaders who are always condemning? They want to be free just the way you want to be free. Do you know those narrow, critical, angry folks in your church? Don't get so mad at them. They would give anything in the world to be free too. Those folks need your prayers and your love.

Everyone Is Afraid

Fourth, the prison keepers and the other prisoners are just as afraid of what you will say and do as you are afraid of what they will say and do.

My friend Fred Smith and I spoke at a conference not too long ago. I had been to this conference center to speak a number of times, but this was Fred's first time. The morning after the first evening's talk, Fred was sitting at breakfast with a man who obviously didn't recognize Fred as the previous night's speaker. Fred seized on the opportunity to get an honest reaction to his speech.

"What did you think of our speaker last night?" Fred asked.

"Well, I haven't decided," the man responded. "He sure was different."

"Know what I thought?" Fred queried.

"Yeah? What?"

"Well," Fred said, "to be honest with you, I thought he was too old and fat."

When Fred came over to my table to tell me what was going on, he was laughing so hard I thought he was going to lose it. "I suspect by now the others at the table have told him who I am," he said. "I'd better get back before he has a heart attack."

Do you know what happens in the church? I'm afraid to tell you what I think and how free I want to be because I'm afraid of what you will think about me and say about me to others. I'll bet most of you are saying, "Really? I thought the same thing about you!" Now . . . we can talk.

It Only Takes One to Start

Fifth, not only are the prison keepers and the other prisoners just like you, not only are there no super-prisoners, not only are they looking for a way out, and not only are they afraid of what you will say and do, but they, just like you, would join the freedom club if someone would just start one.

You know, it only takes one. Early in my ministry I wrote a book about my experiences as a young pastor. (It was titled *Where the Action Is,* and it's out of print, so I'm not trying to get you to buy it.) In that book I told how I had tried to be the leader everyone expected me to be. I tried to be perfect, and it became apparent that I just couldn't pull it off. I was going to have to get honest or get out. I just couldn't live up to all those expectations.

So, with great fear I determined that I was going to be

honest. It was not the most up front and powerfully honest preaching you've ever heard, but it was a beginning, a halting step. Guess what I discovered? That contrary to what I expected, people weren't angry—they were pleased. And even better than that, God's Spirit used my honesty to help them. They responded so positively that I determined to make honesty the basis of my ministry for the rest of my life.

At any rate, I chronicled that experience in the book. Then I started getting letters from other pastors, thanking me for what I had said. Over and over I heard from pastors and laypeople who said how glad they were that someone had finally, in print, given them permission to be honest.

Now, to be perfectly honest, *Where the Action Is* was not a very good book. So why did such a bad book solicit such a positive response? Because it took one person to say it, and pretty soon a lot of good folks who wanted to say it were willing to say it too.

I'm not for a moment suggesting that you run out of the prison and start shouting that you are finally free. You'll only scare those who have the key and don't want to leave. Besides, God almost always works in process. But if you will carefully start talking and living freedom in small ways, you will be surprised at how others will notice and respond. It only takes one.

THE SECRET GOD SHARES

One other thing before we finish this chapter. It is important that we look once again at God. We've had a lot to say about Him and how He feels about our freedom, so we won't go into a lot of detail here. However, I do want you to know that God is not a policeman. He is your

Father. And He is a far different Father than you might have thought.

When I was a junior high school student, we had a principal named Mr. Hunt. He looked like a mean version of "Mr. Clean." He was bald, big, and bad. Everyone (at least the students) was afraid of him. The teachers in that school used Mr. Hunt as a threat: "If you aren't quiet, I will have to call Mr. Hunt," or, "I have just about had it with you. If you don't get better, I'm going to send you to Mr. Hunt's office."

I was sure that the worst thing that could happen to me (short of being thrown off the third floor of the school building) was to have to face the wrath of Mr. Hunt. I tried to be good—really tried but I just couldn't be good enough long enough. The inevitable happened, and I was sent to Mr. Hunt's office. I almost fainted as I walked down the hall to that chamber of horrors, the principal's office.

I knocked very softly on his door, hoping that maybe he was out of his office or that he had died. No such luck.

"Come in," he shouted.

I opened the door but remained in the doorway, fidgeting.

"Shut the door and come in, son," he said. "I won't bite you."

Well, that wasn't what I had heard. I figured he would do far worse than bite me. In fact, I was wondering who would notify my mother of my death.

"Sit down and tell me what you want."

I sat and stuttered something about talking too much in class and Mrs. Smith's sending me for correction. He frowned and I was sure he was thinking of an appropriate punishment for a worm such as me. (Later, I found out that he was frowning because he didn't like Mrs. Smith very much either.)

To my amazement, he told me I probably wasn't as bad as the teacher thought but he did have a reputation to maintain in the school. "If I let you off without any kind of punishment," he said, "then everyone will think I've gone soft. So I'll tell you what I'm going to do."

Here it comes, I thought. *He's going to call the police and they are going to lock me up in a juvenile home for bad boys, and they are going to throw away the key.* I was so engrossed in my fearful thoughts that I heard only the last part of what Mr. Hunt was saying.

". . . and we'll become friends."

"I'm sorry, sir. I didn't hear all you said."

"I said," Mr. Hunt laughed, "that you should tell Mrs. Smith that I was so angry I wanted you to come to my office every afternoon after school. We'll sit around and talk and become friends. I'll make sure our chats don't go so long that you miss the bus."

We did, by the way, become friends. I never told Mrs. Smith what Mr. Hunt had said, and I made a point of looking very sad when I left his office every afternoon—especially when Mrs. Smith was around. I wouldn't talk about what happened with my friends and they just figured, I suppose, that it was too horrible for words. The best part of my day became the time I spent with Mr. Hunt, and I still look back on those times with delight.

God is sort of like Mr. Hunt. But different than Mr. Hunt. God wants us to share the secret.

So now you know the truth my pastor friend and I share. Go knock on the prison door. You might find that no one is there!

CHAPTER 11

A
MATTER
OF
FOCUS
(Focal Points of Freedom)

"Be transformed by the renewing of your mind."
Romans 12:2

Someone tells of the time Gutzon Borglum, the sculptor, was working on the head of Lincoln, which now resides in the Capitol Rotunda in Washington, D.C. The woman who cleaned his studio every evening watched Borglum's work in progress, and soon saw Lincoln's face start to emerge from the marble. She finally asked Borglum, "How did you know Lincoln was in that stone?" It was a matter of focus. She saw the stone, and Borglum saw Lincoln.

If you're looking for holes, the best place to find them is in a screen door. There are thousands of them! It's even possible, I suppose, to be so into holes that you miss the wire that protects the home from insects. Likewise, a lot of Christians never experience the wonderful freedom Christ offers simply because their focus is wrong.

You really can't blame them. The church for the most part has lost its focus too. I'm not throwing rocks—I'm a part of the church and a leader in it. But I have discovered how easy it is to lose focus. After all, there is so much to do—so many problems, so much sin, so many bills to pay, so much structure to maintain. Sometimes, to use a favorite Florida analogy, there are so many alligators we forget to clean the swamp.

The church in general, and Christians, in particular, have a hard time changing focus. Ben Haden, pastor of First Presbyterian Church in Chattanooga, Tennessee, has said that Presbyterians must be very careful to get it right the first time because they are going to be doing it the same way for the next two hundred years. That isn't a peculiar proclivity of Presbyterians; it's a malady from which all Christians suffer. When our focus is set, it is hard to change it.

I want to accomplish a number of things with this book, but some things I know (either from cynicism or experience) I will never accomplish. For instance, I don't expect everyone to read this book. They will perhaps pick it up in a bookstore, read the title, mutter something about easy believism, and put it back on the shelf. I don't expect everyone who begins this book to read this far. They'll become frightened and put it down.

Any talk about freedom does that to some people. They have probably already taken the book back to the store to ask for a refund. Others will hear about the book from those who did read this far and didn't like what they read. They'll say it is a dangerous book because God hates sin and this book, they will say, is a brief for sin. I expect to receive letters from people who want to straighten out my theology and who are concerned about the direction of my thinking.

It's okay. It goes with the turf. I will answer the letters and return the calls and write the responses, but, to be perfectly honest, I don't expect to change very many minds. But they won't change my mind either. Why? Because it's terribly hard to change one's focus.

For those of you, however, who are struggling with the issue of freedom and who have not determined your position, understanding is possible and understanding leads to change. People whose focus is already set in concrete are incapable of change. The reason so many Christians (maybe even you) are still bound by the law is because their focus is wrong. Let's talk about it.

RESULTS VS. RELATIONSHIP

First, we can lose our freedom by focusing on results rather than relationship.

The nineteenth chapter of Acts records a wonderful story. God had used Paul in some miraculous ways; Paul had even cast out evil spirits from those who were oppressed. The seven sons of Sceva saw what happened and decided they would like to be as successful as Paul at exorcism. So they addressed an evil spirit, saying, "We exorcise you by the Jesus whom Paul preaches" (vs. 13). The evil spirit's response would be humorous if it weren't for the pathos of the situation. The evil spirit said, "Jesus I know, and Paul I know; but who are you" (vs. 15)? Luke then gives us a bit of detail: "Then the man in whom the evil spirit was leaped on them, overpowered them, and prevailed against them, so that they fled out of that house naked and wounded" (vs. 16).

The sons of Sceva made a horrible mistake. They focused on the results and the methodology of Paul, rather than on the relationship Paul had with Jesus. We can do that too.

In our presentation of the Gospel we often focus on what Jesus can do for us. Now don't get me wrong. Jesus does a lot for us. He forgives us, reconciles us with God, gives us meaning, and eternal life. But the most important thing about Jesus is He gives us Himself.

We have so emphasized the rewards of following Christ that we have forgotten that following Him, being with Him, knowing Him, and calling Him "Friend" and "Elder Brother" are far more wonderful and important than anything else.

I have found a great way to enhance my prayer life. I have learned to use my imagination (no, I'm not into the

New Age) as I pray for people I love. I used to just tell Jesus what I thought was the problem (as if He didn't know) and enlist His help. Now, in my mind's eye, I picture myself going and taking my friends by the hand up to where Jesus is standing—and then I get out of the way. I am amazed at how many people have told me that their situation changed after I prayed for them.

That's what we need to do.

"If you are with Jesus you will get all kinds of gifts," we tell people when we present Christ. We think if we can get a drunk to Jesus, he will stop drinking—and he probably will. If we can get a mean man or woman to Jesus, Jesus will gentle them, and He probably will. If we can lead a sinner to Jesus, He will change them and make them stop sinning; and, in fact, He does work on that. The problem is that we start to focus on the change rather than the Changer. Unfortunately, by doing that we establish Jesus as a magician who does tricks for His people.

Scott Ross was a popular personality in New York and and a friend of the major rock groups during the sixties. Just after his conversion, Ross said he was thankful people didn't tell him to stop using drugs but, instead, took him to Jesus. I suspect we could take this point too far, but the issue is focus.

We see this problem in the charismatic movement. (I am very favorable to the charismatic movement. I have a daughter who got well because some charismatics prayed for her, so I certainly don't make fun of them—at least not in thunderstorms.) We have seen some wonderful results from the renewed emphasis on the Holy Spirit's power. People have been healed, supernatural power has been manifested, and great numbers of people have come to know Christ. The problem is that it is easy, with that kind of thing happening, to start focusing on the gifts instead of the Giver.

Evangelicals can make the same mistake. We can start focusing on how many people have come to know Christ rather than on Christ Himself. I have a friend who wrote to almost all of the large Christian media ministries asking how many people had been saved during the previous year through their ministry. He commented that according to their statistics, everybody in America had been saved—twice.

There is nothing wrong with results. It's the American way. But when you start to expect those results you can destroy the freedom Jesus gives. It's a wonderful and freeing experience to go to Christ and say, "I'm not here to get anything. I just wanted to be with You. That's enough."

PRODUCT VS. PROCESS

Second, not only can we lose our freedom by focusing on results rather than on relationship, we can (and the second is like the first) lose our freedom by focusing on product rather than process.

That's what happened when John's disciples came to Jesus to ask about fasting. Reading between the lines, you see John's disciples were rather upset about the levity and lack of spirituality among the disciples of Jesus. Jesus answered John's disciples by asking, "Can the friends of the bridegroom mourn as long as the bridegroom is with them" (Matt. 9:15)? When Jesus is present it's time to have a party, and He said that He would never leave us. That makes the process quite bearable. In fact, sometimes the process can be more fun than the goal to which the process is leading.

Most folks have heard the advertising slogan "Getting there is half the fun," or the one that beckons "Adventures in Moving." Well, that's what the Christian faith is all about. When we forget about the adventure of getting there and concentrate on the final outcome, we miss a lot.

I have a colleague who says that the problem with evangelical Christianity is that everybody is selling the product and nobody is using it. We have created a pyramid sales operation, where we either sell the product or teach others to sell it and, honestly, we are moving a lot of product. But nobody is using it.

I saw a sign in the window of our mechanic's shop the other day: "Charges: $10.00 an hour. If you watch: $15.00 an hour. If you help: $20.00 an hour." I suspect God feels the same way sometimes. Too often, we interfere with His work, and we lose our freedom in the process. If we really knew He felt like the mechanic, maybe we would let up a bit and enjoy the abundant life He gives.

One of the most wonderful facts I ever learned was that I didn't have to be God. I used to feel that if I failed, or just let something fall through the cracks, all God planned for the church I served and the people I loved would come to naught. I sometimes think that if I don't act responsibly and if I don't do the right thing, all God's plans for the world will come to a devastating end. Isn't that silly? I'm not God, and He didn't ask me to be His substitute. What a tremendous relief!

"Son," the Father said one day, "for a while do me a favor. Quit trying to help Me. I was doing all right before you came on the scene and I probably won't do so bad after you're gone. So would you let up just a bit?" I did. Nothing came apart. In fact, things got better, and for the first time in my life, I was free.

God works in process. I'm not what I was, but I'm not what I'm going to be either. I'm in the middle of a process. If I remember that, I don't get so frustrated trying to fix everything in my life right now. The church is in a process too. If I remember that, I don't feel the necessity of making everybody feel guilty because they aren't doing what they are supposed to do.

Now I'm not for a moment suggesting that we stop being faithful to the tasks the Father has given. I'm not advocating that we turn from evangelism or service. Remember, it's the focus that counts. It's very easy to start living for the product instead of enjoying living through the process. Jesus is there in the middle of the process, and because He is there, just as He was at the beginning and will be at the end, the middle is just as good as the end and the beginning.

PARTICULARS VS. PRINCIPLES

Third, not only can we lose our freedom by focusing on results rather than relationship and by focusing on product rather than on process—but we can lose freedom by focusing on particulars rather than on principles.

Jesus got ticked at people who put particulars over principles. Listen to His anger: "Woe to you, scribes and Pharisees [Pastors, Elders and Deacons?], hypocrites! For you travel land and sea to win one proselyte, and when he is won, you make him twice as much a son of hell as yourselves. . . . Woe to you, scribes and Pharisees, hypocrites! For you pay tithe of mint and anise and cummin, and have neglected the weightier matters of the law: justice and mercy and faith. These you ought to have done, without leaving the others undone" (Matt. 23:15, 23).

I know a teacher who refuses to use any exam format other than essays. He tells me that anybody can memorize data and put it down on paper with a little effort.

"No," he told me, "I don't care whether or not they know the facts. They'll have to look those up in a book ten years from now anyway. What I want to know in an exam is whether or not the students understand the course."

I think the Father feels the same way. I'm not so concerned about getting the details right. I don't want to lift up a series of rules and expect my congregation to abide by them. However, they do need to understand the principles of the Christian faith.

A number of years ago Anna and I went to Key West, Florida, to visit the home of Ernest Hemingway. We were very interested in seeing where he lived and wrote. A woman guided us through the home, explaining the items in the rooms and how they related to the great writer. Everything went fine until someone asked a question that seemed to upset our guide. Although she answered the question as best as she could, she became quite flustered and afterward started her lecture at the very beginning again. I thought it was just a minor slip until the same thing happened two more times. Each time she broke her concentration on the lecture, she had to start all over. Those of us on the tour reached an unspoken agreement after that: Nobody would ask any more questions lest we end up sleeping in the Hemingway house that night. Our guide had focused so exclusively on the particulars that she couldn't communicate the overall message.

So many Christians live their lives like that. At one time I thought I'd discovered a revolutionary method of marriage counseling that would change the way everybody did marriage counseling. Marriage counselors know that most men are insensitive and that the number one complaint from wives is that their husbands neither share their own feelings nor listen to their wives' feelings.

Well, I decided to teach husbands to be sensitive to their wives. I would say, "On the way home from work today, I want you to think of a feeling you have that you can share with your wife. I want you to stop and buy flowers from one of those corner vendors even if they are Moonies. I want you to tell your wife you love her at least three times before dinner, and I want you to make a point of listening to everything she says after dinner."

Now, doesn't that sound like a great way to get a man to be sensitive to his wife? Wrong! In fact, I created more problems than I solved.

One woman complained, "Pastor, it is like trying to make love with a 'how to do it' sex manual. He comes home and says that he loves me three times. Once he has done that, he feels he has done his duty. I don't feel loved. I feel programmed!"

What I have learned to tell husbands is this: Ask God to give you a deep love for your wife. Think of how you felt when you were first dating. Remember all the ways she loves and supports you. Think of her love for your children and of the things she gives up for them and for you. Remember how she likes to dance and sing. When you have dwelt on that sufficiently, then go home and do what comes naturally.

Read the Bible every morning. Make sure you have a prayer list. Go to church three times a week. Witness to your Christian friends. Serve your church faithfully. Don't drink, smoke, or curse, and don't associate with those who drink, smoke, or curse. Make sure you know doctrine. Volunteer for every project that calls itself Christian. And then, in your spare time, smile a lot, because if you don't, you will hurt your witness.

Don't you get tired of it? I do. Forget it. Forget it all. Just work out the principles of faithfulness, love, patience, and kindness—and then do what comes naturally. I'm not saying that the things I mentioned in the last paragraph aren't important. It's just a matter of focus.

LAW VS. LOVE

Fourth, not only can we lose our freedom by focusing on results rather than relationship, on product rather than process, and on particulars rather than principles, but we can lose our freedom by focusing on law rather than on love.

One of the most astounding statements Jesus ever made is found in the seventh chapter of Luke. Jesus is having dinner in the home of a religious leader when a prostitute breaks in on the party. She anoints Jesus and falls at His feet, washing them with her tears. The religious leaders are shocked and indignant. (Seems we are always shocked and indignant about something.) And then Jesus, rather than putting their minds at rest, shocks them even more: "Therefore I say to you, her sins, which are many, are forgiven, for she loved much. But to whom little is forgiven, the same loves little" (vs. 47).

I know what they thought. Matthew doesn't tell us, but they probably protested, "But Jesus, don't you understand that she is a prostitute? Don't you realize that by accepting her and saying things like that, you are encouraging prostitution? Don't you realize how she has broken the law? Don't you recognize the danger of what you are doing?"

The text doesn't say this either, but I'm sure Jesus looked at the religious leaders with their peacock feathers flying in the breeze. He saw their arrogance and pride as they looked down their noses, and He said, "Shut up! Just shut up!"

Are laws important? Of course, they are. But it's a matter of focus. If I have time to tell people either how to be good or how to love Jesus, I don't even question which to say. If they love Him and mess up everything else, it's no great loss. If they don't love Him and do everything else right, they can lose eternity.

(By the way, you learn to love Him by allowing Him to love you. You can't love until you have been loved, and then you can only love to the degree to which you have been loved. Love isn't something you just "do," because you can't do it until you've got it. Love starts by just being still [it's okay, God doesn't need your help] and letting Him love you. We know that we are called to love others, but a lot of those others are twits. How do you love a twit? How can you show love to the unlovely? Let me tell you: You get the love from the source, and then you will have it to give away. That isn't my idea. Check 1 John 3:16 and 4:10.)

FANTASY VS. FACTS

Fifth, not only can we lose our freedom by focusing on results rather than relationship, on product rather than process, on particulars rather than principles, and on law rather that love, but we can lose our freedom by focusing on fantasy rather than fact.

The Bible is very clear about the fallen nature of the world. It's not a pretty picture. I am constantly amazed at how Christians can become Pollyanna almost without thinking. They say, "Isn't the world grand! Isn't everything wonderful! Isn't life fine! Isn't it great to be a Christian!" I want to say something kind and pastoral to those kinds of people like, "Are you some kind of fruitcake or what?"

We live in a fallen world (Gen. 3). That means that things aren't grand. But more important, you and I aren't grand either.

Have you ever found that the good becomes the enemy of the "not half bad"? It happens, you know. We live in a very messed up world, and very little, if anything, is perfectible this side of heaven. If that is true, and you spend all of your time expecting perfection—or what is close to perfection—either in yourself or in others, you are going to be miserable, dishonest, or neurotic. Thus, it is sometimes important to rejoice in the "not half bad."

If your son or daughter gets a B instead of the A you expected, you say, "You can do better than that!" instead of, "That's not half bad." When your pastor preaches a fairly good sermon, you say, "Didn't have time to prepare this week, Reverend?" instead of, "That's not half bad." When your wife has been up to her ears in kids all day, and, given the circumstances, has prepared a fairly good meal, you say, "Tomorrow I hope you have more time to fix dinner," instead of, "That's not half bad." When your husband comes home after a fight with his boss (which was the best thing that happened all day), and he kisses you on the cheek and heads for the easy chair, you say, "You can do better than that," instead of "That's not half bad." When your wife is trying to work at her job and maintain her sanity by being your wife too, you say, "Looks to me like you could organize yourself better," instead of, "Honey, I appreciate how hard you work."

You get the idea.

Let me give you one of the working principles of the universe: When a dog plays checkers, don't criticize its game. Be pleased and surprised that the dog is playing at all. In other words, in a fallen world don't expect a whole lot. When you get anything good, you ought to be pleased. Or to put it the way I've put it in the front of my Bible: "You wouldn't be so shocked by your own sin if you didn't have such a high opinion of yourself."

I'm not saying that Christians shouldn't strive for excellence. But I am saying, for God's sake, try to be more realistic about the way you are and the way the world is. It's a matter of focus.

JUDGMENT VS. JESUS

Finally, not only can we lose our freedom by focusing on results rather than relationship, product rather than process, particulars rather than principles, law rather than love, and fantasy rather than facts, but we can lose our freedom by focusing on judgment rather than on Jesus.

I love Jesus' words concerning tax collectors. When He was criticized for spending time with such riffraff, He responded, "Those who are well have no need of a physician, but those who are sick. But go and learn what this means: 'I desire mercy and not sacrifice.' For I did not come to call the righteous, but sinners, to repentance" (Matt. 9:12–13).

The other day I listened to the confession of a pastor who had done some terrible things. Because of his actions, he had been kicked out of his church and was now living with a considerable amount of shame and remorse. As I listened to his story, I found myself loving him. He didn't make excuses, but as he talked, I could see the trap he had fallen into. Through his tears he cried, "I know I don't deserve it, Steve, but do you think God could ever use me again?"

"Of course God can use you again," I replied. "He

loves you more than you will ever know. He has already forgiven you and is even now planning how He is going to use your sin for His glory and you for His service."

Do you know how I felt? Guilty. I started thinking to myself, *Myself, you are only trying to make him feel better, and you dare to speak for God. This is a man who has violated all the rules, and you are letting him off easy. What if he hasn't repented sufficiently and you bring condemnation not only on him, but on yourself by not telling him the truth?*

And then God spoke (in Hebrew, of course) through my knowledge of Scripture. "Stephen, are you out of your mind? If you can love him, don't you think I can love him? If you can understand, don't you think that I can understand?

"You've given him your time. . . . I gave him My life!"

If we spend a lot of time telling people about their sin—how they have failed and how they could do better—they are going to become discouraged. Not only that, they will continue to fail, and they will refuse to get better. Besides, most people are already painfully aware of their sin, of how they have failed and how they ought to get better.

Just tell people about forgiveness, and then get out of the way. The devil will take the hindmost, and God will continue the process. The results will be far better than you would ever believe.

Am I saying we should not tell people about the horror of sin? Of course not. Am I saying we should not teach biblical methodologies of getting better? No way. Am I saying we should encourage failure? Are you kidding? All I'm saying is that it's a matter of focus.

William Holman Hunt, English painter and founder of the Pre-Raphaelite brotherhood, took his students outside to paint the sunset. As one young man worked furiously on his canvas, Hunt noticed he was painting a barn.

"Son," Hunt said, "you can paint that magnificent sunset or you can paint that barn. It will be dark soon and you don't have time to paint both."

Hunt's comment was apt for Christians as well as the artist. Certain things about the Christian life are important, and certain other things are far more important than the ones that are important. If we focus on the less important, we will build a prison for ourselves and for others that will rob us of our freedom. You can focus on rules, regulations, propriety, and programs for righteousness; or you can focus on Christ and your relationship with Him. You can hardly do both.

Prisons are only for people who think it's important to live in them. What about you?

CHAPTER 12

PERMISSION
TO
BE
FREE
(The Doorway to a New Life)

*"Now the Lord is the Spirit; and where the
Spirit of the Lord is, there is liberty."*
2 Corinthians 3:17

I overheard some people talking about my ministry the other day. That's dangerous business because God is gracious, and He usually only lets you hear the bad stuff. But on this occasion He allowed me to overhear a visitor talking to a church member and, for once, I was glad to hear it. The visitor was having trouble describing our church. (Someone has said that Miami's ecclesiastical picture is like a grid with different shaped holes. Those who are round go to one church, those who are square go to another, and those who are rectangular go to still another. Those who are left go to our church.)

The visitor had made some very positive comments about the church and wondered why the church was so different. Our member responded, "The secret is that our pastor has given us permission to be free."

Sometimes I get letters from pastors who say, "Steve, you seem so free in the things you say and do. You must have a lot of courage." I would like to say that I am particularly brave and courageous for the Lord. If I did, I would be lying. I am freer than most pastors, but not because I'm brave. Rather, I manifest a high degree of freedom in my ministry because the congregation I serve has given me permission to be free.

What a wonderful situation. Cynics may say after as many years as I have served the Key Biscayne church, I know so much dirt about the congregation, and they know so much dirt about me, that we have a standoff.

They may say we allow each other to be free because neither wants the other to reveal the dirt. Not so.

As a matter of fact, we have discovered a secret. Everybody wants to be free in Christ. But very few people realize that everybody wants to be free in Christ, so most of us play a game. We conform to what everybody thinks everybody thinks, and we end up imprisoned by our own fear. If somebody has the courage to say, "Hey, you guys. I'm tired of playing this game. I just can't keep this up anymore," you would be surprised at the response. If just one person had the courage to say it, everybody would find out what everybody else really thinks, and we would start giving each other permission to be free.

That's what has happened in the church I pastor. We've been free so long I don't even remember who was free first. But whoever the person was, he or she did us all a favor. And the freedom is wonderful.

Giving people permission to be free is one of the most exciting concepts imaginable, and I want to share it with you in this chapter. If, after reading this chapter, you courageously decide to give people permission to be free, you will be blessed not only by the Father but by your Christian friends as well.

Can we talk?

THE FORM WITHOUT
THE POWER

You and I both know that so often the church is probably the last place in the world where people are really free. We talk about freedom, we preach it and offer it to those who have not found Christ. But if you take a long look around the average church you will find people who seem to be cut from the exact same mold.

I once heard a humorist who had just been to Disney World say how impressed he was with the bright, excited, pleasant, enthusiastic young people who worked there. He wondered how Disney had been able to find that many young people with such good attitudes. He decided that there must be a gigantic freezer on the back lot of Disney World where they kept frozen kids from the fifties. When they needed a new employee they simply went to the freezer and thawed one out. He concluded that Disney was going to be in trouble when they ran out of frozen fifties kids.

Well, someone could almost say the same thing about the church. I can usually spot a Christian at fifty paces. Do you know why? Because most of us look, act, and talk the same way.

Now don't get me wrong. The standard Christian is not a bad type. He or she might even be a rather pleasant sort with an aura of freedom. When you first meet one, you might even say that person is free. But then you meet another one, and another one, and pretty soon you begin to wonder where the factory is.

There is, of course, a cold, dead orthodoxy among us which we have called "Christian." Paul warned Timothy to be careful about those who "have a form of godliness but deny its power" (2 Tim. 3:5).

We can get so interested in right doctrine, right living, and right worship that we lose the power of Christ and become a cold, formal, proper, pure mausoleum.

Jesus made a very important statement about those kinds of churches: "No one puts a piece of unshrunk cloth on an old garment; for the patch pulls away from the garment and the tear is made worse. Nor do they put new wine into old wineskins, or else the wineskins break, the wine is spilled, and the wineskins are ruined. But they put new wine into new wineskins, and both are preserved" (Matt. 9:16–17).

Jesus hates dull, proper gatherings about as much as you do. In fact, He spoke rather strongly about the matter: "Woe to you, scribes and Pharisees, hypocrites! For you are like whitewashed tombs which indeed appear beautiful outwardly, but inside are full of dead men's bones and all uncleanness" (Matt. 23:27).

Do you know why Jesus hates cold, formal, proper, pure mausoleums? Because they become masks behind which we can hide our own insecurities and failures.

Did you hear about the congregation who had terrible trouble with their pastor's angry, narrow sermons? In the town barber shop one day the barber asked one of the church elders if they had been able to remove the minister. "No," the elder replied, "we've decided to keep him." In answer to the barber's surprised look the elder added, "We got to talking and decided that as a service to the Body of Christ we needed to keep him. If we fired him he would go to another church. If he went to another church, they might listen to him."

I feel sort of like that about the kinds of churches I've described above. They will eventually die off and nobody will even notice. I'm not talking about them as much as I'm talking about Christians who seem to be free, who belong to churches who sing upbeat contemporary songs, who smile a lot, and put on a friendly atmosphere. This kind of church fosters a feeling of freedom, but the rules are very strong and you don't know about them until you break one. This kind of church encourages, then cajoles, then is harsh, and then turns its back on "out of line" Christians. This kind of church is the most dangerous because the manipulation is so subtle.

I met some kids the other afternoon who were so alive

and free that I wondered what had happened to them. They laughed and talked with me on the street corner. They used "God words" and I assumed they were Christians. But when I asked them about their beliefs, I was surprised to find that they were members of one of the most manipulative, devastating cults in America. I watched them get on their bus after their street witnessing. They were all smiles. They were a lot like some Christians I know. I was reminded of the "Stepford Wives," and I wanted to cry.

Let's talk about giving permission to be free. If you decide to be God's significant instrument in the cause of real freedom, how do you go about it?

YOU NEED TO BE FREE

First, I suggest that you get free. Freedom isn't something you can share if you aren't free yourself. Until you see it, you can't show it. That sounds like a truism, but it really isn't. Violin players who think they can play the violin and can't, sound like dying cats. Swimmers who think they can swim and can't, drown. Christians too often use words without understanding their meaning just because the words are "Christian" and Christians are supposed to use Christian words. Freedom is an important Christian word, so we must be careful not to use it in our conversations, unless we have it.

There is nothing more dangerous to the cause of Christian freedom than for someone who knows nothing about freedom to talk about it to others. In fact, that's one of the major problems with the whole idea of freedom. I once worked for a radio station where the program director decided to play an April Fool's joke on our audience. All the station personalities had to write and produce a commercial that didn't sell a product. We were asked to find the right musical "bed" and to describe a sale or special reduction using adjectives like *gigantic, colossal,* and *wonderful.* We could talk about the product that came in a variety of colors and a wide range of sizes. The trick was that we were never to mention a product.

Guess what? We all produced our commercials and aired them, but no one noticed. We didn't get a single call about our commercials! Nobody even paid the slightest bit of attention.

That can happen to Christians too. The late Vance Havner, one of our nation's greatly loved Bible teachers, said that the difference between Jesus and us is that we advertise and don't produce; He produced and didn't advertise. If you're afraid ever to go against the crowd, to say something that doesn't sound Christian, to offend people, to bask in the glorious acceptance of Christ, then for His sake don't talk about freedom. If you are bound by rules and regulations and if you never ask questions or express doubts, please don't tell anyone about freedom. If you aren't free, don't proclaim freedom. Pagans will get the idea that you illustrate the message and go back to their own cells—which aren't a whole lot worse than yours.

Remember when Jesus read the Scriptures in the synagogue? He said He had been sent to "proclaim liberty to the captives . . . and to set at liberty those who are oppressed" (Luke 4:18). He then demonstrated the freedom He proclaimed.

He broke the religious rules, touched the untouchable, loved the wrong people, and offended the right ones. He didn't say what everyone expected, and He refused to capitulate to the forms that would enslave Him. Above all, He kept on loving, even on a cross.

Ask Jesus to make you free. It is His gift of love to you. And after He gives it to you, then you can give it to someone else. How can you give it away? How do we give each other permission to be free?

I would like to say that I have learned to give people permission to be free because I'm so spiritual, but if I said that you might talk to my wife. To be perfectly honest, one of the best ways to be free yourself is to allow others to be free. Let me share with you what I've learned.

Be Responsible for Yourself—Not Everyone Else

First, I don't have to be God to anyone else. Remember what happened in Lystra with Paul and Barnabas? You'll find the story in the fourteenth chapter of Acts. God had used Paul and Barnabas in a wonderful way, and the people of Lystra (including the priest of the temple of Zeus) thought they were gods. When Paul and Barnabas realized what was happening, "they tore their clothes and ran in among the multitude, crying out and saying, 'Men, why are you doing these things? We also are men with the same nature as you'" (vv. 14–15).

I understand how Paul and Barnabas felt, and I'll bet you do too. People love to have others make decisions for them. It is human nature to find someone you love and respect and to ask them to guide and help you. I remember feeling that way when I went to Frank Jean (a Chinese missionary to America). As a young pastor, I was tired of having to always be wise, understanding, and strong. So I went to Frank. "Frank," I said, "I need a pastor. Will you be my pastor?"

We were having lunch in Boston and I will never forget the surprised expression on his face. He was kind but firm. "Stephen," he said, "I can't be your pastor. God is your pastor."

Was Frank making an anti-pastor statement? No. Looking back I understand. He recognized in me a proclivity to let someone else make my decisions and take my risks, and Frank refused to do what only God was supposed to do.

The people who come to me for pastoral counseling are often surprised when I say, "I want to be your friend, and I will be your pastor. I will hurt when you hurt and I will cry with you. I will teach you what God says in His Word. I will pray for you and I will love you—but I will not be your mother. If you are looking for a mother, you have come to the wrong person."

Now that may sound harsh, but it isn't. I'm reminding them that I'm not God. And if I'm not God, I'm not responsible for doing things for people that only God should do. What a great emotional relief. And perhaps more important, people begin to face the responsibilities of being free Christians and to accept the implications of their own decisions.

I have a poster titled "Basic Training (for living in your office, your home, or anywhere in the world)." The philosophy expressed is not half bad:

> If you open it, You close it.
> If you turn it on, You turn it off.
> If you unlock it, You lock it.
> If you break it, You repair it.
> If you can't fix it, You get someone who can.
> If you borrow it, You return it.
> If you use it, You take care of it.
> If you make a mess, You clean it up.
> If you move it, You put it back.

If you make the promise, You keep it.
If you don't know how it works, Don't touch it.
If it doesn't concern you, Don't mess with it.

The "you-do-it" philosophy is just another way of saying that we give others permission to be free when we refuse to shoulder other people's responsibilities. Taking responsibility for others is a form of ego-centered control that imprisons both them and us.

Be Honest

Second, I refuse to be dishonest with my brothers and sisters in Christ. Paul gave this advice to the Ephesians: "Therefore, putting away lying, 'Let each one of you speak truth with his neighbor,' for we are members of one another" (Eph. 4:25).

I am committed to honesty in two ways. First, I am honest about who I am. That doesn't mean I feel called to confess all my sins in detail before every Christian I meet. But it does mean that I must not pretend to be more spiritual and righteous than I am—that I must not put on a mask of godliness for the benefit of my spiritual family. I am committed to telling you the truth about me, thereby giving you the freedom to tell me the truth about you.

I remember one time when a man I had put on a spiritual pedestal confessed his sins to me. I was absolutely devastated. I thought, *Don't do this to me. I need a hero, and you're the only one I have left.* But he insisted on telling me his sins. He said I was looking at him improperly and he felt uncomfortable with it. "Steve," he told me, "if we are going to be friends, it is important that you know something about your friend."

Know what? He's the person around whom I feel the most comfortable. Our relationship is extremely honest, and when I'm around him I feel free.

But there's another side to this honesty business. Honesty requires me to be honest with you about what God says about you and you be honest with me about what God says about me. One of the problems with relational theology is that it often degenerates into excuses for disobedience: If I'm bad and you're bad, then it must not be so bad to be bad. May God have mercy on us.

I told a friend of mine the other day who was thinking about divorce, "Jerry, I'm not sure what I would do in your place. It's hard for me to understand all you face without living in your skin. But I am responsible before God to tell you what God says about divorce. Once I have told you, you are then responsible for your own decision. I will still be your friend whatever you do, and I will still love you, but you need to know that God hates divorce." He is my brother, and I owe him the truth.

A man told me once that he was having trouble discerning God's will about his mistress. I didn't lie to him. I told him that discerning the will of God in that particular matter was relatively easy, given the fact that God had spoken so clearly and often on the subject. Truth demands that I never hedge when speaking to members of my spiritual family.

Allow Others to Bear Their Own Guilt

Third, I refuse to bear the guilt for someone else's sin. (Now I recognize that there is a sense in which we share in each other's guilt as did Nehemiah in his prayer for his people. However, that is another subject altogether.) We each must do our own business with God. Listen to the words from Ezekiel 18:20: "The soul who sins shall die. The son shall not bear the guilt of the father, nor the father bear the guilt of the son. The righteousness of the righteous shall be upon himself, and the wickedness of the wicked shall be upon himself."

Manipulators have an unbelievable ability to bring others into their guilt. One of the things that I have learned from Alcoholics Anonymous is that people with a booze problem are not the only ones who are sick. Those who live with them often have a disease too: guilt. "Where did I go wrong?" is a common question for members of an alcoholic's family. Alcoholics help the process, too, since generally they are looking for someone else to blame.

I have often seen this need to transfer guilt in calls from people who are contemplating suicide. Do you know what I often say to someone who tries to manipulate me with a threat of suicide? I say, "Look, don't put that trip on me. If you decide to commit suicide, that is a totally selfish act, but it is your act and your decision. If you do it, I will feel sorry, but I want you to understand that I will not feel guilty. So you can forget about trying to make me feel that way."

Of course, I say more than that. I am not so cruel and heartless that I won't show love, understanding, and concern. But I have found it necessary to stake the proper territory before giving help.

Parents, your kids are not computers you have programmed. You are not responsible every time there is a glitch. Don't let your adult kids get away with making you responsible for their actions ("Look at what you have caused in my life"). Pastors, don't bear the guilt of the people to whom God has sent you. Only Christ can share

213

their guilt. If you try to do what only Christ can do, you will spend all your time feeling guilty. Christians, love does not dictate that you feel guilty every time locusts attack the crop in a Third World country or (closer to home) a Christian friend doesn't live up to your expectations. Tell those who try to make you walk down that road, "I refuse to be guilty for your actions. I will love you, but I won't bear your sins. You have to do that by yourself or, as a pleasant alternative, allow Christ to bear them for you."

How horrible! No, it really isn't. When we refuse to bear another's guilt, we give them permission to be free. How so? We have made a statement about their personal responsibility. Their unhealthy dependence on others to affirm and share in their guilt is a horrible form of slavery.

Allow People to Be in Process

Fourth, I have learned to think of people as living in process. Jesus said to His disciples, "I still have many things to say to you, but you cannot bear them now" (John 16:12).

A friend who is studying to be a therapist told me once about how she was learning to relate her counseling to freedom. Let me quote from her letter: "I am trying to learn to be a good therapist and they keep telling me that I have to help the clients come to their own conclusions and decisions. If I give them an insight before they are ready, they are not likely to act on it, and I may even slow the process of self-discovery and change. Therapists seem to agree without question that true change only comes when the client sees an insight for herself (himself) and makes his or her own choice. The therapist has to wait it out, even when the client makes poor choices, because the real goal in therapy is not to make the clients dependent on us to make decisions, but to help the clients make their own good decisions. True strength and true growth only come from having gained the insight oneself and having chosen freely. The therapist has to see that gaining strength is often more important than making a good decision at the moment."

Now that's not always my method in counseling. I'm usually more directive than that. However, my friend's words are highly insightful for relationships among Christians. We are not willing to allow people to be where they are in their own process. We want them to be where we are, and we are quick to do everything in our power to get them there. By recognizing that everyone is in a process and that God is in charge of the process, and by refusing to get in the way of the process, we give people permission to be free.

Don't Be Shocked

Fifth, I refuse to believe that there are any super-saints for whom Christ did not have to die. The Bible says that all have sinned and fallen short of the glory of God. If that is true, and I haven't found any exceptions yet, then I will not be shocked by the discovery that all have sinned and fallen short of the glory of God.

Let me tell you something that may shock you. There is no sin of which I am not capable. In other words, I can do anything that anybody else has done, both good and bad. I love the little boy who prayed, "Dear Jesus, forgive all the bad things I did today, and forgive all the bad things I thought about but didn't get around to doing." Unless I am capable of committing the sin you are committing, I am not capable of being anything but your judge. You don't need a judge—you need a friend.

Any reasonably intelligent, aware pastor, who has been a pastor more than a year, won't be shocked by anything. I think I've become shockproof. People always think that what they are going to tell me will cause me to faint dead away. The truth is that I have heard the same story (whatever it is) so many times I could probably save some time in counseling sessions by giving a summary of the problem before the person tells me about it. By not being shocked, we give people permission to be free.

Let People Be Human

Sixth, I have learned to recognize what it means to be human. I'm so tired of hearing about the victorious Christian life that I think I will die. Do you know what the victorious Christian life is? It is keeping your nose above water. It is keeping on trucking for another day. It is being faithful—just barely. It is keeping from messing it up too terribly. We have this idea of what a real Christian ought to be, say, and think, and then we try to live up to that idea and force everyone else to live up to it too.

A number of years ago I was speaking at a religious emphasis week at a Christian college. Shortly before I went to speak at the college, a woman I had known for a number of years died. She had been one of Christ's most faithful servants. Her witness had literally touched thousands of people in some exciting and positive ways.

Her daughter was a student at the college and one evening after the meeting I noticed her standing in line waiting to speak to me. I was interested in what she was going to say. When she got up to me, she said, "Mr. Brown, I'm Sara Clark (not her name)."

"Sara," I said, "I knew your mother, and I loved her. She was an inspiration to so many of us. I know this must be a difficult time for you."

"Not at all," she said smiling. "I know where my mother is. She is in heaven, and her funeral was a witness to how our family is praising God. We saw a number of people come to know Christ at the funeral. Don't waste any pity on me. I'm a Christian."

With uncharacteristic bluntness (well, maybe a little characteristic), I said, "Sara, don't give me that kind of balderdash. If your mother's dead and you're happy about that, you're not playing with a full deck."

Do you know what happened? She fell apart. The tears flowed for the first time in weeks. Sara and I spent a lot of time together that week talking about her mother, how she loved her, and how much she missed her. Most of the time I just let her talk and cry and be angry. She had found someone who allowed her not to be "Christian" for a change, someone who didn't reject her honest feelings.

Sara is doing fine now. She still misses her mother. She knows that her mother is with Christ, and Sara has a much stronger witness to her friends now because it is honest and free.

The point? Sara had been given a set of standards that as a Christian she felt she must maintain. One of those standards was that Christians praise God all the time and never deal with tragedy honestly lest they hurt their witness for Christ.

By allowing people to be human, we give them permission to be free.

Grace Is Enough

Finally, we give people permission to be free by understanding that if grace is good enough for God, it ought to be good enough for us. "For by grace you have been saved through faith, and that not of yourselves; it is the gift of God, not of works, lest anyone should boast" (Eph. 2:8–9).

One time a teacher promised my daughter a high grade on a course she was taking in high school. She made the promise because the teacher wanted to help my daughter understand that the purpose of the course was not to get a good grade, but to learn something important. As we have mentioned before, the grade has already been given to you. It happened on the cross and you received an "A." When we give permission to others to be free, we have properly transferred the same process to them. If you got an unearned "A" you ought to be willing to give your brothers and sisters an unearned "A" too.

Grace is not just something God has shown us, it is something that we must show others.

And so we come to the end of our study in freedom. Please don't write me letters telling me that Christian freedom is not only "freedom from" but "freedom to." I know that and I meant to say something about it. There just wasn't room. We'll have to save it for another book.

The problem I see is that so many Christians are caught in a trap of Christian bondage that "freedom to" is not even an issue. If you are trapped in seaweed fifteen feet under the water and drowning, you can't swim until you get free from the seaweed.

But if you are free, you will find that you have another kind of freedom, and that is the freedom to be obedient to the One who gave you your freedom. If you haven't discovered that, you simply haven't gone far enough for the fun.

Remember the first miracle Jesus ever performed? You'll find the story in the second chapter of John. It was a party and the host ran out of wine. Jesus turned the water into wine and thereby saved the day. If you're a Christian, Jesus has given you the wonderful, heady, exciting wine of freedom.

Be sure you do not turn it back into water.

NOTES

1. *Encyclopedia of Religious Quotations,* Frank S. Mead, ed. (Westwood, NJ: Revell, 1955), 275.

2. C. S. Lewis, *The Weight of Glory and Other Addresses* (New York: MacMillan, 1965), 104.

3. Gerald Kennedy, *With Singleness of Heart* (o.p.).

4. Martin Luther, "Letter to Melanchton," quoted in *Encyclopedia of Religious Quotations,* 407.

5. Allan Bloom, *The Closing of the American Mind* (New York: Simon and Schuster, 1987), 142, 151.

6. D. M. Lloyd-Jones, *Romans, An Exposition of Chapter 6, The New Man* (Grand Rapids: Zondervan, 1973), 9–10.

7. Stephen R. Donaldson, *The One Tree* (New York: Ballantine, 1982), 21.

8. *The Hymnbook* (Philadelphia: John Ribble, 1950), 12.

9. John Calvin, *Institutes of the Christian Religion,* Chapter II, Section 43 (Philadelphia: Westminster Press, 1960).

10. F. F. Bruce, "A Mind for What Matters," *Christianity Today,* April 7, 1989, 24.

11. C. S. Lewis, *The Last Battle* (New York: MacMillan, 1956), 147–148.

12. Charles Spurgeon, *Lectures to My Students* (London: Passmore and Alabaster, 1875).